WITHDRAWN

CALCULATORS IN THE CLASSROOM: with applications for elementary and middle school teachers

DAVID G. MOURSUND
University of Oregon

contributing editor
DOUGLAS L. SHULT

JOHN WILEY & SONS
New York   Chichester   Brisbane   Toronto

Library of Congress Cataloging in Publication Data

Moursund, David G.
  Calculators in the classroom.

  1. Programmable calculators.   2. Mathematics—
Data processing.   I. Shults, Douglas L., joint author.
II. Title.
QA75.M75   510'.7'8   80-22165
ISBN 0-471-08113-2

Printed in the United States of America

10 9 8 7 6 5 4 3 2 1

CONTENTS

PREFACE

This book has been written with several purposes in mind. First, it serves as an introduction to calculators—how they work and what their capabilities and limitations are. Considerable care has been taken to explain calculator logic, digit and screen display, calculator functions and programs, four-key memory, and calculating procedures. Calculator limitations are discussed, and the differences between calculator arithmetic and paper-and-pencil arithmetic in the real number system are presented. Frequent exercise sets not only build proficiency in calculator manipulation but also provide a broad understanding of calculator functions and uses.

The second purpose is to help elementary and middle school teachers to apply calculators in classroom settings. A variety of suggestions and applications appear throughout the text. This material is not organized by grade level. Instead, it is presented in such a way that teachers can adapt it to their specific needs.

Third, the book is intended to provide teachers with insights into the potential impact of calculators on the school curriculum. Emphasis is placed on problem solving. Steps in problem solving are examined, and the relationship of calculators to this process is fully explored. Functions, formulas, and flowcharts are discussed, and calculator applications to these topics are presented. Extensions of the mathematics curriculum are implied through discussions of large numbers, decimal equivalents, and number patterns. A concluding section on calculators and computers describes the relationship of calculators to computers, their distinguishing characteristics, types of problems appropriate for each, and the eventual effect computers will have on the school curriculum.

The book contains ample preparation for teachers who want to begin making instructional use of calculators. It has been written from a mathematical perspective, but it does not assume knowledge of mathematics beyond a modern eighth-grade level. The text can be used in a self-instruction mode or in an ordinary classroom setting with other preservice or inservice teachers. In any case, it is to be studied with a calculator in hand. For most purposes the least expensive four-function pocket calculator will do; however, if you intend to purchase a calculator, it is recommended you first read Chapter 2.

Exercise sets are designed for teachers, although slight modifications make many problems appropriate for students. Chapters 6 and 7 contain classroom application sets. Problems in these sets are specifically designed to be used with students. Selected numerical answers for both types of exercises appear at the end of the text. Also, at the end of the book, there are several appendixes and a glossary. Appendixes cover the metric system, calculator usage in schools, and a review of calculator research, while the glossary provides useful definitions of words and terms used in the text.

The book is short and organized in small increments. The Table of Contents is complete including a breakdown of references, appendixes, and related back matter. In the interest of saving space and expenses we have eliminated an index.

You should study the book from cover to cover. Begin by browsing through it. Then, return to Chapter 1 and dig in. You will soon be immersed in a new world— the world of electronic aids to problem solving.

We thank C.L. (Cheri) Shirts for her technical assistance in the design and layout of the text and Percy Franklin for his artwork.

DAVID MOURSUND

In The Beginning . . .ONE

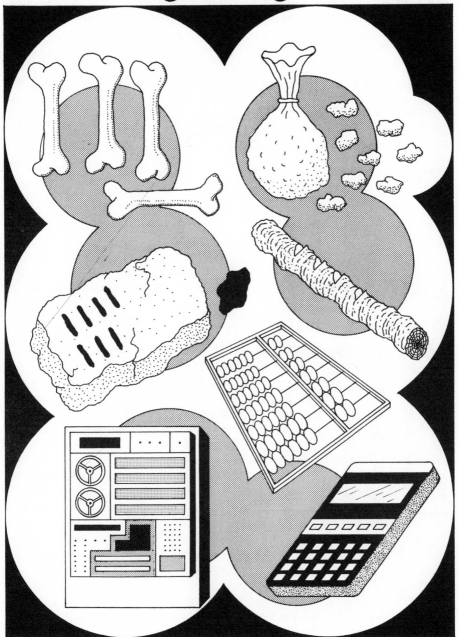

More important, there are alternative methods of calculation. For example, one might use a book of mathematical tables. Given below is a small part of such a table. From it one can read that the square root of 23 is 4.795832.

Portion of a Table of Square and Square Roots

n	n²	√n		√10n
20	400	4.472	136	14.14214
21	441	4.582	576	14.49138
22	484	4.690	416	14.83240
23	529	4.795	832	15.16575
24	576	4.898	979	15.49193

In recent years the electronic calculator has become readily available. Common estimates are that a calculator can be found in about 95% of the homes in the United States and that about 30 million are purchased annually in this country. Many of these calculators have a square root key, labeled √ . To calculate the square root of 23, one merely keys the number 23 and then the √ key. In less than a second the answer is displayed.

The concept illustrated in this example is important. Square root is an important idea in mathematics and occurs frequently as one applies mathematics to solve "real-world" problems. Thus, it is an appropriate topic for a mathematics curriculum. But what should the student learn? Is it worth the student's time and effort to master a *paper-and-pencil* computational algorithm for determining square root? Or, might the student learn the concept, meaning, and use of square root, and some alternative computational method? Specific to the thrust of this book, should the student be allowed to use a calculator? Answers to these questions will become clear as you progress through the book.

Critics of our educational system often claim that it takes 50 years to implement a significant change in education. But a revolution is now brewing that will have a massive impact in a much shorter time span. This revolution is based upon electronic technology — calculators, computers, and videodiscs. The changes that will occur are as profound as those produced by the invention of movable type and the mass production of books.

It is often difficult to see the forest when one keeps bumping into trees. To understand the electronic-based revolution in education, one needs to understand both the individual components — calculators, computers, videodiscs, etc. and how they interact with education. The next quarter century will witness massive change to both the content and process of education. This book is designed to help prepare you to participate in the changes that have already begun.

1.1 A Simple Example

You know that the (positive) square root of 9 is 3, since $3 \times 3 = 9$. Similarly, the square root of 49 is 7. What is the square root of 23?

You should be aware that there is a major difference between the concept, or meaning, of square root and knowing how to calculate a square root. In essence, these are two distinct topics. At some stage of your past education it is likely that you studied an algorithm, or recursive procedure, for calculating square root. Perhaps it was the algorithm illustrated below:

```
          4. 7 9   Etc.
        | 23.000000
          16
    87 |  700
          609
   949 |   9100
          8541
           559
```

This algorithm is considerably more complicated than those typically used for long division. Most likely if you ever did learn it, by now it is forgotten. Most people master such complicated algorithms only by repeated use. How often do you find a need to calculate a square root?

1.2 Why A Whole Book?

A calculator is a marvelous device. Even a child can learn to use one in a few minutes, with little or no instruction. Thus, a calculator is easy to use and is easy to learn how to use.

Why, then, do we need an entire book on calculators in elementary and middle-school education? It is because there is more to calculators than merely punching a few keys to perform a calculation. Read the questions given below and see how many you can answer. By the time you finish this book you should feel comfortable in dealing with questions such as these.

1. Define the following terms:

    overflow   floating point arithmetic
    underflow   scientific notation
    RPN   function
    algebraic logic   eight-digit calculator
    LCD   problem
    LED   truncation or rounding error

2. Explain how a four-key memory system works, illustrating by explaining its use in calculating with fractions.

3. Explain the role of calculators in problem solving. Do this by outlining the major steps or phases of problem solving.

4. Explain similarities and differences between real arithmetic and calculator arithmetic.

5. Give at least five examples of how to use a calculator to enhance learning of traditional elementary school mathematics topics.

6. Discuss similarities and differences between calculators and computers. Give examples of types of problems most suited to each.

1.3 Calculators and Computers

A calculator employs the same type of electronic circuitry used in computers, and the two types of machines are closely related. Indeed, there is no fine dividing line between calculators and computers.

Some "fancy" calculators, those which contain many function keys and/or are programmable, cost more than the least expensive microcomputers. Such hand-held calculators have capabilities that rival those of full scale, room-sized computers of the late 1940's.

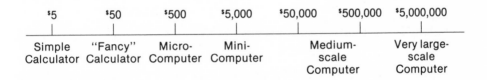

$5	$50	$500	$5,000	$50,000	$500,000	$5,000,000
Simple Calculator	"Fancy" Calculator	Micro-Computer	Mini-Computer	Medium-scale Computer		Very large-scale Computer

In this book you will gain considerable insight into what calculators can do. You will also come to understand their educational implications. The square root example is roughly in the middle-range of calculator capabilities. Addition, subtraction, multiplication, division, and simple memory features occupy the lower range. On the higher side there are trigonometric, exponential, and logarithmic functions; larger memories; and programmability.

Each topic presently taught in the mathematics curriculum needs to be examined in light of calculators and computers. Because elementary school mathematics currently places a great deal of emphasis on the four basic arithmetic operations, it is here that calculators may have the greatest impact.

1.4 Now It's Your Turn

This book is divided into many small sections which often end with exercises. Mathematics is not a subject one can learn by merely reading the material once or twice. Math is learned by doing math — by sweating over exercises. As a general rule of thumb, you should look at each exercise. If it is immediately evident how to do the exercise, then there is little value in doing it. But if you can't immediately see how to do an exercise, *then* the exercise is worth doing. It is in doing such exercises that most learning will occur.

Mathematics is traditionally thought of as an individual activity best performed by people who are "brains" and "recluses". This need not be the case, especially at the elementary school level. There is considerable educational research showing that working in pairs enhances learning in a wide variety of subject matter areas. Working with another person can help to make math more humane and enjoyable — and you may even learn more.

Keep in mind, of course, that the goal is to learn to do mathematics. In the exercises, getting the answer is not the main goal. Rather, the goal is to learn to solve a particular type of problem or to better understand a key idea.

Exercise Set 1.4

These exercises are suitable for discussion in class or in small groups. Alternatively, they may be done as written exercises. Select one of these methods and answer the following questions:

1. What is mathematics? What does it mean to "know" mathematics? Compare your answers with those of a colleague. How are your answers similar? How do they differ?

2. How does one communicate knowledge of mathematics? Illustrate by communicating some major aspects of your mathematical knowledge. That is, what mathematics do you know?

3. The mathematics curriculum in many elementary schools progresses in a systematic fashion year by year up to the problem of long division of decimal numbers, which first may be encountered in the sixth grade. For many students this appears to be a dividing line or major branching point. Those who master this topic proceed into an accelerated mathematics track beginning in the seventh grade. Those who don't are put into a slower or remedial track, often never to emerge. This inability to master a particular paper-and-pencil calculation strongly influences the remainder of a student's formal education.

The electronic calculator has a relatively short history. In 1965 the first electronic calculator was produced. It was about the same size and price as the desk model electromechanical calculator it was designed to replace. Approximately $170 worth of transistors and other electronic components were hand-assembled to make this $1500 machine. It was faster and quieter than electromechanical calculators.

Progress in electronics and in the computer field led to the integrated circuit and later to the large-scale integrated circuit. The first "chip," measuring less than a centimetre on a side, contained only a few dozen transistors and related components. Now "chips" contain thousands of microscopic circuits. Because of these and other advancements in technology and automation, the components in the original electronic calculator costing $170 were replaced by smaller, more efficient parts worth a few dollars.

The hand-held calculator, as we know it today, became commercially available in the early 1970's. By the mid-1970's the price of a simple four-function calculator was about the same as a college level textbook. These inexpensive calculators quickly became as commonplace as TV sets, and as calculators became cheaper, their use in elementary and middle schools increased.

The Case for Using Calculators in Schools:

Studies dating back to an investigation by Emmett Betts in 1937 show that students can successfully operate calculating machines in the elementary grades with no loss of computational ability. Further studies report that students who use calculators can make significant gains in achievement of concepts and computational ability over students who do not use calculators. Other research claims that calculators do not hinder motivation for learning mathematics, nor do they act to negatively influence the development of positive attitudes toward mathematics learning.

The National Council of Teachers of Mathematics (NCTM) studied the appropriate role of the calculator in the mathematics curriculum, and in 1974 NCTM adopted the following position statement, giving formal endorsement to the use of calculators in classrooms:

"With the decrease in cost of the minicalculator, its accessibility to students at all levels is increasing rapidly. Mathematics teachers should recognize the potential contribution of this calculator as a valuable instructional aid. In the classroom, the minicalculator should be used in imaginative ways to reinforce learning and to motivate the learner as he becomes proficient in mathematics."

Notice that NCTM used the term "minicalculator" to refer to the hand-held calculator discussed in this book.

To further clarify the NCTM position, the Instructional Affairs Committee of the National Council of Teachers of Mathematics (NCTM, 1976) identified several basic justifications for the use of hand-held calculators in mathematics classrooms. Among them were the following:

1. To encourage students to be inquisitive and creative as they experiment with mathematical ideas,
2. To reinforce the learning of the basic number facts and properties,
3. To develop the understanding of computational algorithms,
4. To serve as a resource tool that promotes student independence in problem solving,
5. To be used to solve problems that previously have been too time-consuming or impractical to be done with paper and pencil, and
6. To decrease the time needed to solve difficult computations. (p. 72-74)

In 1975 the National Science Foundation (NSF) funded an investigation to critically analyze the role of the calculator in precollege mathematics programs (Suydam, 1976). The study was designed, in part, to identify the range of beliefs and reactions regarding calculator use in schools and to identify the arguments in support of incorporating calculators within the school mathematics curriculum. The most frequently cited reasons for using calculators in schools, as stated by teachers, state supervisors of mathematics, mathematics educators in colleges and universities, and textbook publishers were summarized by Bell, Esty, Payne, and Suydam (1977) (p. 230-231) as follows:

1. They aid in computation. They are practical, convenient, and efficient. They remove drudgery and save time on tedious calculation. They are less frustrating, especially for low achievers. They encourage speed and accuracy.
2. They facilitate understanding and concept development.
3. They lessen the need for memorization, especially when used to reinforce basic facts and concepts with immediate feedback. They encourage estimation, approximation, and verification.
4. They motivate. They encourage curiosity, positive attitudes, and independence.
5. They aid in exploring, understanding, and learning algorithmic processes.
6. They encourage discovery, exploration, and creativity.
7. They help in problem solving. Problems can be more realistic, and the scope of problem solving can be enlarged.
8. They exist. They are here to stay in the real world; so we cannot ignore them.

A further discussion of the advocate position on the use of calculators in schools is contained in Appendix B. Also in this appendix, you will find an outline of the opponent's point of view and a presentation of ways school districts are using calculators.

Research on Using Calculators in Schools:

The 1970's saw a rapid growth in research on the use of calculators in education. To collect, summarize, and disseminate this research information and other material on calculators in education, the United States government funded the Calculator Information Center at Ohio State University. The center issues information bulletins and reference lists throughout the year on topics such as types of calculators, selecting a calculator, books on calculator applications, and research references on calculators — precollege level.

A research review of calculator effects on attitudes, achievement, computational skills, and problem-solving ability of precollege students is presented in Appendix C. A careful reading of this review will give you a general understanding of the types of research that are being done, the questions researchers are asking, and the results of their research.

An alternative, of course, is to give students calculators. Discuss the general statement of the preceding paragraph in light of this alternative.

4. In mathematics you have learned that one "can't divide by zero." Why can't one divide by zero? Suppose that you divide by zero on a calculator. Will this break the machinery? Try it.

> Well, doctor, it began when I was in 4th grade . . . long division . . .

1.5 Math Anxiety

People with a high level of math anxiety generally avoid math whenever possible, and have little confidence in their ability to learn math. In recent years math anxiety has been extensively studied by psychologists, learning theorists, and mathematics educators.

There are a variety of causes of math anxiety. For some students math anxiety begins as they first encounter multidigit multiplication. Others find that decimals or long division give them fits. Just the thought of adding fractions may be enough to petrify some students. In certain cases a calculator can help overcome math anxiety. With a calculator in hand a student can perform a long division calculation as rapidly as adding a pair of numbers.

As a teacher it is important that you be aware of math anxiety. You want to help prevent its occurrence in your students, and/or help alleviate it when it does occur. An excellent starting place is with yourself. As you study mathematics, try to examine your feelings. Be aware when you are becoming anxious or confused. When you can't learn something, try to figure out why. When you are ready to throw in the towel on your math studies, examine why you are upset. What do you find particularly frustrating? Do others have the same difficulties?

Exercise Set 1.5

1. What does the term "math anxiety" mean to you? Give examples of how it manifests itself in you or in someone you know.

2. Think back to your own elementary school mathematics experience. Recall a situation in which math was fun, and you enjoyed it. Next, recall a situation in which math was not fun for you. Compare the two situations. What do you conclude about learning and teaching math and about yourself?

3. Select a person, preferably a child, who seems to have a high level of math anxiety. Write a brief case study of this person's encounter with mathematics. Include in your report the source of math anxiety and/or when it began, experiences which continually cause anxiety, view of self as a math learner, self concept in a broader sense, and hope for future success in mathematics.

4. Select a person, preferably a child, who seems to have a low level of math anxiety. Write a brief case study of this person's encounter with mathematics. Examine apparent success with math, view of self as a math learner, self concept, and plans for future involvement in mathematics.

5. Compare your case studies obtained in Ex. 3 and Ex. 4. Write a report on your findings.

6. Interview several people, preferably children, who seem to have high levels of math anxiety and several who seem to have low levels of math anxiety. From your findings make several general statements about the possible sources of math anxiety, activities or experiences which produce math anxiety, the effect of math anxiety on a person's self concept and view of self as a math learner, and the relationship of math anxiety to future plans for math study. How do these general statements compare with the results of your case studies?

1.6 History of Aids to Computation

We conclude this chapter with a brief historical overview of calculators. This will give you some perspective of their current role in education.

Mankind's earliest written records include examples of enumeration. Counting aids such as stones in a bag, notches in a stick, and tally marks made with charcoal are lost in antiquity. Such inventions led to the development of counting boards and abacus-like devices approximately 5000 years ago.

For thousands of years people have worked on the task of developing improved aids to computation. One outcome of their effort is the Hindu-Arabic numeral system we currently use. Ideas such as the 0, positional notation, and the decimal point represented major breakthroughs. Imagine the difficulty of trying to learn procedures to multiply or divide Roman numerals.

Another early aid to computation was mathematical tables. If a particular problem occurs frequently, one can record its solution. A simple example is provided by a table of multiplication facts. Other examples include navigational tables, astronomical tables, and artillery firing tables. The concept represented by a math table is very important. Most people using a table are not interested in the detailed computation that went into creating the table. Rather, they view it as a quick and accurate way of securing an answer to a difficult computational problem. They make use of this computational aid in solving higher-level problems, such as navigating across the ocean.

Considerable insight into the progress of developing computational aids can be gained by examining the early 1600's in Europe. In 1617 John Napier published a paper describing the use of "rods" or "bones" to perform multiplication and division of whole numbers. Use of Napier's rods allows multiplication and division problems involving whole numbers to be done using only addition and subtraction. This was important because, at that time, multiplication and division were considered to be topics one studied in college. Many well-educated people of the time could not solve multiplication and division problems.

John Napier also developed logarithms. Their use allows multiplication and division calculations involving decimal numbers to be done using addition, subtraction, and logarithm tables. Logarithms provide the mathematical theory underlying a slide rule and were very valuable computational aids to scientists and engineers until quite recent times. Calculators and computers have diminished this importance.

In Europe during the early 1600's people began to experience success in building mechanical calculating machines. Current historical records give credit to Wilhelm Schickard for developing the first successful machine in 1623. Although Schickard's machine could add, subtract, multiply, and divide, it did not receive wide attention. Blaise Pascal, a famous mathematician, received considerably more credit for the calculator he built in 1642. It could add and subtract. In 1671 Gottfried Leibniz built a machine that could add, subtract, multiply, and divide. This was a good machine, and ideas from it have been used in building mechanical calculators until modern times. It wasn't until 1820, however, that such machines became commercially available.

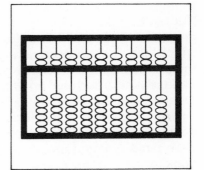

The history of computation is a history of progress in seeking better aids to computation. The goal has been to develop inexpensive, reliable, universal aids so that the ability to calculate would not be restricted to the intellectually elite. In Europe during the 16th century, the Hindu-Arabic numeral system which we currently use finally prevailed over other systems. Paper-and-pencil algorithms were developed for multiplication and division and began to be widely taught. As western European countries chose to emphasize paper-and-pencil computations, use of the abacus disappeared. The abacus, however, is such a good aid to computation that it continues to be used in many parts of the world.

For most people there was little progress in the development of aids to computation from 1600 until quite recently. The mechanical calculators that were developed were fairly expensive and not readily available. Their existence had little or no impact on education. A major change during the 1800's was the development of cheaper methods for making paper. Thus, chalk and slate which was used prior to the 1800's gave way to pencil and paper as an inexpensive medium for recording the steps in carrying out computations.

Of course, work continued in the development of better machines — machines that were more reliable, faster, more automatic, and easier to use. When electricity and electric motors became available, people began to use them in calculators. In the late 1800's the electro-mechanical calculator was developed as a competitor to handcrank machines. At about the same time, Herman Hollerith seized upon the idea of using punched cards for data processing. The 1890 United States census data was recorded on 63,000,000 punched cards and processed using tabulating machinery he developed. Out of Hollerith's work grew the punched card data processing industry and International Business Machines (IBM).

Serious work on developing full scale electrically-powered computers began in the 1930's. First such work was directed toward building machines using telephone-type electrical relays. A relay is merely a switch that is controlled by an electromagnet. Then, to gain increased computational speeds, vacuum tube circuitry was developed. During the early 1940's, significant progress occurred in several countries. In England Alan Turing designed a computer-like machine which was used in deciphering German World War II secret codes. In the United States a machine called the *ENIAC*, built at the University of Pennsylvania, became operational in December, 1945. This vacuum tube machine is generally considered to be the first general purpose electronic digital computer. The first commercial electronic digital computer was the *UNIVAC I*, produced in 1951. Progress since then has been rapid. Computers are discussed briefly in the last chapter of this book.

The ENIAC Computer

Exercise Set 1.6

1. Examine a recent issue of the *Arithmetic Teacher.* Comment on the nature and quantity of articles and ads dealing with calculators. (Note that the entire November 1975 issue was devoted to calculators in elementary education.)

2. Examine a modern elementary school mathematics book designed to be used in the fifth or sixth grades. Comment on the nature of how calculators enter into this book. Compare and contrast your findings with your answer to Ex. 1.

3. Make a list of arguments *against* the use of calculators in the elementary school. From this, select your one "best" argument *against* the use of calculators at this level. Then, write a counterargument.

4. Make a list of arguments *for* the use of calculators in the middle school. From this list, select your one "best" argument *for* the use of calculators at this level. Then, write a counterargument.

5. Use the information you developed in Ex. 3 and Ex. 4 to help you prepare a debate for presentation in class on a topic of your choice having to do with calculator use in schools. Select a colleague as your opponent. Present either the pro-argument or the con-argument with your colleague presenting the opposite position. Discuss the outcome of the debate in class. Three possible topics are:

   ● Calculators *should be used* freely in the elementary (or middle) school for all purposes.

   ● Calculators *should be used* in the elementary (or middle) school for limited purposes only.

   ● Calculators *should not be used* in the elementary (or middle) school for any purpose.

6. There seem to be five general-use patterns in school districts which use calculators (see Appendix B). Select any two of these, and give the possible advantages and disadvantages for students in these programs.

7. From your analysis of the research studies given in Appendix C, what dimensions of a student's mathematical behavior seem to be most affected by a calculator. Substantiate your answer by reference to specific studies.

TWO

Calculators: to know them is to use them

scientists and engineers working in research and industry. Generally, RPN caluulators contain a number of trigonometric function keys and other features not suited to the elementary or middle school.

Eight-digit, Floating Decimal Point: Some inexpensive calculators can handle only numbers up to six digits in length. More common is the eight-digit calculator, which can calculate and display an answer as large as 99,999,999. Some pocket calculators display up to 10 digits, while many desk-top business calculators display 12 digits. Calculators which display eight digits are adequate for most elementary and middle school work.

On most such calculators the decimal point "floats". That is, the decimal point positions itself automatically to make full use of the calculator's accuracy. On an eight-digit floating-decimal-point calculator, one finds:

$$10 \div 3 = 3.3333333$$
$$100 \div 3 = 33.333333$$
$$1000 \div 3 = 333.33333$$

Contrast this with a fixed decimal point machine. For example, suppose the calculator is constructed to display only two places to the right of the decimal. On such a machine one finds:

$$10 \div 3 = \quad 3.33$$
$$100 \div 3 = \quad 33.33$$
$$1000 \div 3 = 333.33$$

More expensive calculators, often called slide rule calculators, use scientific notation. A number is represented as a decimal fraction times an appropriate power of 10. For example, 8,240 is expressed in scientific notation as 8.24×10^3. On a slide rule calculator 8,240 appears as 8.24 on the left of the display screen with 10^3 on the right. Since scientific notation is generally not taught until the seventh grade or later, such calculators are of little use in the elementary school. However, for some highly motivated and advanced middle school students, slide rule calculators may provide the appropriate motivation for extended mathematical and scientific inquiry.

Screen display: The least expensive calculators use a lighted screen to display numbers, while more expensive machines may print answers on a paper tape. A paper tape printout is essential to many business applications, but is not necessary for most school uses.

Two types of screen displays are common: the light emitting diode and the liquid crystal display. The light emitting diode (LED) is very visible in dim light, since the display actually consists of small lights. A

The four-function algebraic-logic pocket calculator is amazingly easy to use. Suppose you wish to compute 82.4 + 67.83. After turning on the calculator you simply key from left to right ⑧ ②　． ④ ⊞ ⑥ ⑦ ． ⑧ ③ ⊟ . The calculator stores this information in its memory, carries out the calculation, and displays the answer of 150.23.

Unfortunately, all calculations are not this simple. Many require a variety of complicated steps. In addition, there are many different kinds of calculators. Some have extremely complex keyboards that demand considerable effort to understand. It is also easy to make errors using a calculator, so one must learn to detect errors as well as avoid them. This chapter provides an introduction to the things you need to know in order to make effective use of a calculator.

2.1 What Kind of Calculator?

There are dozens of different brands of calculators on the market, and many are suitable for use while studying this book. However, the great majority of calculators currently being sold have certain features in common. These features are stressed here. If you do not yet own a calculator, it is suggested you buy one with the features discussed below. Such a calculator will meet all computational needs of typical elementary and middle school students.

Algebraic Logic: An algebraic-logic calculator accepts numbers and operations in the order they appear in horizontal mathematical notation. For example, to do the problem 6 + 4 = one simply keys ⑥ ⊞ ④ ⊟ and the answer 10 is displayed. One of the most important keys on an algebraic-logic calculator is the ⊟ key. Pushing that key tells the calculator to perform the calculation using the operation and numbers that have been keyed in.

Reverse Polish Notation: A common alternative to algebraic-logic is reverse polish notation (RPN). Calculators employing reverse polish notation do not have an ⊟ key. To add 6 to 4 one keys ⑥ ⎣ENT⎦ ④ ⊞ and the answer is displayed. The ⎣ENT⎦ key (enter key) is used to enter numbers into a calculator memory. A calculator using RPN is particularly well suited to many of the mathematical problems faced by

set of batteries may last eight to 12 hours in a LED calculator. Liquid crystal display (LCD) depends upon reflected light for its visibility. Thus, the display is difficult or impossible to read in dim light. The battery drain in a LCD calculator is minimal, so a set of batteries may last 1,000 to 2,000 hours or more.

Since LED uses batteries more rapidly than LCD calculators, manufacturers are gradually moving toward the use of liquid crystal. Most schools also prefer LCD over LED calculators because of battery replacement, and thus the operating expense, becomes a very minor problem.

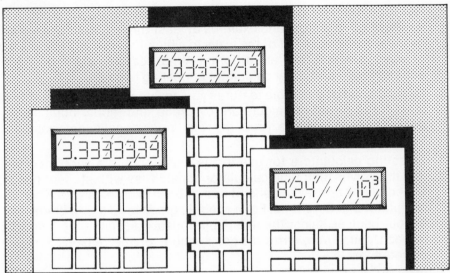

Four-, Five- or Six-function: A four-function calculator can perform the functions of addition, subtraction, multiplication, and division. A common fifth function is √ (square root) and a common sixth function is % (percent). Some calculators have dozens of additional built-in functions, such as trigonometric functions, statistical functions, or certain common business-oriented functions. All of these are beyond the needs of elementary and middle school students.

Four-key Memory: Many calculators have some "extra" memory and four keys to use the memory. The M+, M−, RM, and CM keys are very useful in working with fractions and in certain other relatively complicated calculations. Chapter 5 is devoted to this topic. On some calculators the CM key is combined with the C key, but overall the calculator functions just like the four-key memory machine discussed in this book.

Exercise Set 2.1

1. Like every academic discipline, the calculator field has its own vocabulary. Part of learning mathematics is to learn the vocabulary and to make it part of your everyday, working knowledge. Without referring back to the book, explain the meaning and purpose of the following terms:

   a. Screen display   e. Eight-digit display
   b. Algebraic logic   f. Floating decimal point
   c. LED   g. Fixed decimal point
   d. LCD   h. Scientific notation

2. Get together with two people whose calculators are different from yours, or go to a store and examine at least three distinctly different calculators. Make a list of the ways in which they are alike, and a list of ways in which they are different. What features seem desirable and/or make a particular calculator appealing to you?

3. Using the list of desirable features you developed in Ex. 2, identify at least three different calculators by brand and model number that possess these features. From the retail price of each, determine the best buy. Disregard sale prices.

4. Selecting calculators for use in the classroom is a very important job. It involves matching calculator capabilities with student needs. Listed below are seven pairs of items. Each pair deals with a certain calculator characteristic. For a specific grade level (i.e., a grade level of your choice), select the most appropriate calculator characteristic in each pair. Then, write a brief account of the reasons for your preferences.

   a. Eight-digit display   d. Floating decimal point
      10-digit display   Fixed decimal point
   b. Algebraic logic   e. Four-key memory
      Reverse polish notation   No memory
   c. Four-function   f. Display digits 1cm high
      Six-function   Display digits 1.5cm high
                                g. Calculator the size of a
                                      credit card
                                   Calculator the size of a billfold

5. From the list of appropriate characteristics you developed in Ex.4, try to identify at least three different calculators which feature most of these characteristics. Considering retail prices of each, determine the best buy. Also, try to determine whether dealers are willing to give discounts to schools for large orders.

6. Most calculators have a $\boxed{C}$ key and a $\boxed{CE}$ key, although they may be combined into a single key. By experimentation and/or reading your calculator's instruction manual, learn the purpose of the clear key and clear entry key. Then explain the purposes in your own words, making the differences quite clear.

7. On some calculators the $\boxed{=}$ key possesses a "repeating" function. Find a calculator with such a characteristic, and by experimentation and/or reading the instruction manual, learn to use the "repeating" $\boxed{=}$ key. For what purposes can this feature be used in elementary and middle school math programs?

2.2 Simple Calculations

One of the appealing features of a calculator is that it is easy to learn how to use. Even a first grader can learn to turn it on and perform a simple arithmetic calculation. Usually, only a minute or two of instruction is required for an adult who has not previously used a calculator to learn how to add, subtract, multiply, and divide on it. This book assumes that you have already mastered a calculator at this level. Test yourself, and your calculator.

$$
\begin{array}{r}
97.6 \\
142.8 \\
76.2 \\
+\ 379.7 \\
\hline
696.3
\end{array}
\qquad
\begin{array}{r}
82.94 \\
\times\ 61.7 \\
\hline
5117.398
\end{array}
\qquad
894\overline{)\begin{array}{r}3921. \\ 3505374.\end{array}}
\qquad
\begin{array}{r}
897.46 \\
-\ 98.78 \\
\hline
798.68
\end{array}
$$

Did all of your answers come out the same as the book's answers? Think of some reasons why this might not be the case. (Be sure to allow for the possibility that the book is in error!)

The first thing one should do after turning on a calculator is to make certain it is working correctly. A few simple tests should be run to give you confidence that the machine is functioning properly. Some typical tests are given below.

1. Does the display work? On most screen display calculators the value 0. is displayed when the calculator is turned on. Divide 10 by 9 to fill the display with 1's.

2. Does each digit key work? Key in ①②③④⑤ and check the display. Push the Clear key, which is ⒸC or Ⓒ/CE on most calculators. This should return the display to 0. Then, key in ⑥⑦⑧⑨⓪ to check these digit keys.

3. Next, perform some simple computations to check the four functions +, −, ×, and ÷. In each case perform a calculation you can do mentally. Then, mentally check your calculator's answer.

4. Finally, check out the other functions or features you plan to use. For example, does the calculator have a square root key? If so, then ① ⑥ √ should produce 4.

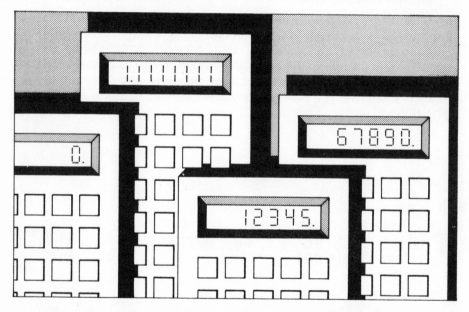

These simple tests will detect most major malfunctions that occur with calculators, but there is no guarantee that all hardware bugs (i.e., flaws in circuitry performance) will be detected. Your calculator might calculate 2 × 3 = 6 correctly and yet still give an incorrect answer to 239.8 × 62.47. One cannot have absolute confidence in the performance of a calculator. If the power supply is working and the calculator passes the simple tests given above, then very likely it is functioning correctly.

Exercise Set 2.2

Exercises 1 through 4 in this set can be adapted easily for use with students. If you have a group of students available, give them these exercises and compare your conclusions with theirs.

1. Test your calculator to see if it seems to be working correctly. Explain why it is not possible to fully test a calculator to guarantee that it is working perfectly.

2. Given below are two sixth-grade-level "mathematics competency" tests. Do Test A using pencil and paper. Time how long it takes you. Then do Test B using a calculator, timing yourself again. Check your answers by using the Answers section at the end of this book. Write a brief report on how your paper-and-pencil computational speed and accuracy compares with your calculator computational speed and accuracy.

Test A.

(1)   932
    $\times\ 7$

(2)   8664
    $-\ 3273$

(3) $30\overline{\smash{\big)}7020}$

(4)   54
    $\times 20$

(5)   115
       47
       53
       19
       82
        6
        8

(6) $6\overline{\smash{\big)}9865}$

(7) $89 + 7 + 25 =$

(8) $85{,}423 - 2{,}798$

(9) 30×570

(10) $604 \div 4$

Test B.

(1)   815
    $\times\ 6$

(2)   3785
    $-\ 1394$

(3) $40\overline{\smash{\big)}6080}$

(4)   31
    $\times 30$

(5)   200
       73
       62
       18
       91
        7
        5

(6) $5\overline{\smash{\big)}6729}$

(7) $77 + 8 + 306 =$

(8) $68{,}873 - 4{,}678$

(9) 40×460

(10) $804 \div 3$

3. Here are two groups of 20 number-fact problems. Do the first group *mentally.* Work rapidly but carefully. Record your time and number of errors.

5 + 4 = ☐	7 − 2 = ☐	8 × 2 = ☐	6 ÷ 6 = ☐
3 + 8 = ☐	9 − 3 = ☐	3 × 7 = ☐	24 ÷ 8 = ☐
10 + 5 = ☐	10 − 6 = ☐	4 × 2 = ☐	7 ÷ 1 = ☐
3 + 7 = ☐	13 − 8 = ☐	6 × 5 = ☐	36 ÷ 6 = ☐
12 + 5 = ☐	14 − 7 = ☐	7 × 4 = ☐	42 ÷ 7 = ☐

Do this next group using a calculator. Key in *each calculation* and record the calculator answer. Give your time and number of errors.

7 + 2 = ☐	9 − 3 = ☐	7 × 3 = ☐	8 ÷ 8 = ☐
9 + 3 = ☐	8 − 5 = ☐	5 × 6 = ☐	30 ÷ 5 = ☐
10 + 7 = ☐	10 − 6 = ☐	2 × 9 = ☐	63 ÷ 9 = ☐
5 + 6 = ☐	14 − 9 = ☐	5 × 7 = ☐	42 ÷ 6 = ☐
13 + 4 = ☐	16 − 8 = ☐	8 × 4 = ☐	54 ÷ 9 = ☐

What conclusion can you draw from this experiment?

4. Here are some calculation problems. Decide which method *you* would use to solve them. Label the problem with:

   M mental arithmetic   P paper and pencil   C calculator.

   Work rapidly. Do not actually carry out the calculations.

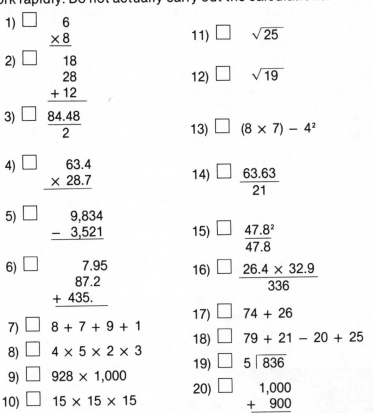

1) □   6
        × 8

2) □   18
        28
      + 12

3) □ 84.48
      ─────
        2

4) □   63.4
      × 28.7

5) □   9,834
     − 3,521

6) □   7.95
        87.2
      + 435.

7) □ 8 + 7 + 9 + 1

8) □ 4 × 5 × 2 × 3

9) □ 928 × 1,000

10) □ 15 × 15 × 15

11) □ √25

12) □ √19

13) □ (8 × 7) − 4²

14) □ 63.63
       ─────
         21

15) □ 47.8²
       ─────
        47.8

16) □ 26.4 × 32.9
       ──────────
          336

17) □ 74 + 26

18) □ 79 + 21 − 20 + 25

19) □ 5 ⌐836

20) □   1,000
      + 900

Now look back and analyze your responses. Write a brief report on your conclusions.

5. Select a grade level. As carefully as possible answer Ex. 4 from the perspective of a student at that grade level. How do these answers differ from your own?

6. From the results of the experiments you conducted in Ex. 2 through 5, write a brief statement reflecting *your* thoughts on the roles of mental arithmetic, paper and pencil, and the calculator in carrying out numerical computations at both the elementary and middle school levels.

2.3 Order of Operations

What is 3 + 2 ÷ 5? One way to interpret the question is (3 + 2) ÷ 5. Another way is 3 + (2 ÷ 5). Depending upon the interpretation, one gets either 1. or 3.4 as an answer. To a mathematician such ambiguity, or lack of precise meaning, is not tolerable. And, of course, such a situation is a serious problem for calculator manufacturers.

Key in ③ ⊞ ② ⊡ ⑤ ⊟ on your calculator. Do you get 1. or 3.4? The answer you get depends upon the brand of calculator you are using! A sequence of calculations, such as in this problem, is called a chain of calculations, or simply a chain calculation. It is important to learn how your calculator and other calculators handle chain calculations.

You should be aware that *people* created the symbols, such as 3, + , 2, ÷ , 5, and = appearing in a chain calculation. Thus, it is people (namely, mathematicians) who make up the definitions stating the precise meaning of the symbols. When a student studies mathematics the student must learn the notation and its precise meaning.

Mathematicians have agreed upon a rule for chain calculations. This rule is called the *hierarchy of calculations.* It states that each computation within a chain of calculations must be performed in a definite order and in a prescribed manner. The order is summarized as follows:

1. Parentheses
2. Powers
3. Multiplication and division
4. Addition and subtraction

Examples below more fully illustrate the order of calculations and the manner in which they are computed. It is important that you learn the *hierarchy of calculations* and understand its meaning.

Parentheses: These always occur in pairs. A computation is performed beginning with the innermost pair of parentheses and working outward.

$$(7 \times (3 + (16 \underset{\downarrow}{\div} 4) - 5)) \div 2$$
$$(7 \times (3 + \underset{\downarrow}{4} - 5)) \div 2$$
$$(7 \times \underset{\downarrow}{2}) \div 2$$
$$\underset{\downarrow}{14} \div 2$$
$$7$$

Powers: These are to be evaluated as they are encountered, while working from left to right in an arithmetic expression.

$$\underset{\downarrow}{5^2} + \underset{\downarrow}{2^3} - \underset{\downarrow}{3.5^2}$$
$$25 + 8 \underset{\downarrow}{-} 12.25$$
$$20.75$$

Multiplications and Divisions: These are to be evaluated as they are encountered, while working from left to right.

$$8 \underset{\downarrow}{\div} 2 \times 6 \div 3 \div 2$$
$$4 \underset{\downarrow}{\times} 6 \div 3 \div 2$$
$$24 \underset{\downarrow}{\div} 3 \div 2$$
$$8 \underset{\downarrow}{\div} 2$$
$$4$$

Addition and Subtraction: Work from left to right and evaluate them as they are encountered.

$$6 \underset{\downarrow}{+} 9 - 5 - 3 - 6 + 17$$
$$15 \underset{\downarrow}{-} 5 - 3 - 6 + 17$$
$$10 \underset{\downarrow}{-} 3 - 6 + 17$$
$$7 \underset{\downarrow}{-} 6 + 17$$
$$1 \underset{\downarrow}{+} 17$$
$$18$$

Recall the example used to begin this section. According to the *heirarchy of calculations,* we have

$$3 + 2 \div 5$$
$$\downarrow$$
$$3 + .4$$
$$\downarrow$$
$$3.4$$

But, the majority of inexpensive calculators will give 1. for the calculation

$$\boxed{3}\ \boxed{+}\ \boxed{2}\ \boxed{\div}\ \boxed{5}\ \boxed{=}$$

Thus, to get the correct answer it is necessary to (mentally) rearrange the calculation. That is, one (mentally) inserts parentheses so that the calculation becomes 3 + (2 ÷ 5). This is then keyed into a calculator as

$$\boxed{2}\ \boxed{\div}\ \boxed{5}\ \boxed{=}\ \boxed{+}\ \boxed{3}\ \boxed{=}$$

By a little experimentation with chain calculations you will see that with most calculators it is not necessary to key $\boxed{=}$ except at the end. The above problem is solved correctly by $\boxed{2}\ \boxed{\div}\ \boxed{5}\ \boxed{+}\ \boxed{3}\ \boxed{=}$. You will gain more insight into the use of the $\boxed{=}$ key when you study Chapter 5 on calculator memory.

Exercise Set 2.3

Mathematics educators generally agree that about three-fourths of all calculations most people need to perform can be done mentally. Mental arithmetic skills can be improved with practice. Do each of the following problems mentally. Then verify your answers using a calculator.

1. Using the *hierarchy of calculations*, perform the following computations.
   a. $(3 \times 4) - 8$
   b. $12 - (4 \times 2)$
   c. $(26 \div 2) + 9$
   d. $3^2 - (4 \times 2)$
   e. $4 \times (8 + 7) \div 2$
   f. $(8 \times 7 + 4)/15$
   g. $((12 + 9 \div 3) + 4^2) \times 2$
   h. $(16 \div 2^2) + 3 \times (8 - 5)$

2. Insert parentheses where necessary into the following expressions so that the calculations can be done according to the *hierarchy of calculations*. Then perform the computations.
   a. $7 + 3 \times 8$
   b. $32 - 4 \times 7$
   c. $75 \div 3 + 2$
   d. $37 + 10^2$
   e. $8^2 - 24$
   f. $6 \times 7 \div 21$
   g. $3 \times 8 + 6$
   h. $21 + 48 \div 8$
   i. $6^2 \div 2 + 8$
   j. $13 + 3^2 - 12$

k. $7 \times 3 + 16 \div 4$
l. $9 - 7 + 4^2 \div 2$
m. $12 + 2^2 \div 4 - 12$

n. $11 - 8 + 12 \div 3 \times 2$
o. $8 \times 3 - 4 \times 2 + 7^2$
p. $26 - 5 + 2^3 \times 8 \div 4$

3. Find the missing number in each of the following equations.

a. $\boxed{} \times 17 = 51$

b. $4 \times \boxed{} + 5 = 37$

c. $6 \times \boxed{} - 24 = 30$

d. $\boxed{} \div 10 + 72 = 172$

e. $9 \times 8 - \boxed{} = 40$

f. $500 \div \boxed{} - 20 = 0$

4. Use a systematic method of trial and error to find solutions for the equations below. Each equation may have more than one solution. Remember: a solution is a number that, when substituted for $\boxed{}$ in an equation, makes the left side equal to the right side.

a. $\boxed{}^2 + 2 \times \boxed{} = 3$

b. $3 \times \boxed{}^2 + \boxed{} = 30$

c. $\boxed{}^2 + \boxed{} = 56$

d. $\boxed{}^3 - \boxed{} = 60$

e. $\boxed{}^4 + 8 \times \boxed{} = 105$

5. Calculate answers to **a** through **d** below. Then examine your answers, looking for a pattern. Try to guess the solution to **e**. Check using a calculator.

a. $3^2 - 2^2$
b. $5^2 - 4^2$
c. $6^2 - 5^2$
d. $10^2 - 9^2$
e. $73^2 - 72^2$

6. In order to test a calculator a student wants to find the sum: $\frac{1}{2} + \frac{1}{2}$. The student keys

$\boxed{1}\ \boxed{\div}\ \boxed{2}\ \boxed{+}\ \boxed{1}\ \boxed{\div}\ \boxed{2}\ \boxed{=}$

and gets .75 as an answer. Explain why.

2.4 Getting Right Answers

You have some arithmetic calculations to perform. You have tested your calculator and it seems to be working correctly. Will you get the correct answers?

Not necessarily. There are too many things that can go wrong. For example:

1. You might read the numbers or operations in a calculation incorrectly.
2. You might make a keying error.
3. You might make an order-of-operation error.
4. A key might stick, or a twitch in your finger might cause you to (incorrectly) depress a key twice.
5. The battery may run down, causing the calculator to function incorrectly.
6. You might read an answer incorrectly.

Many of these types of errors are easily detected, provided only that you continue to use your brain and eyes as you use a calculator. The following suggestions will help you to detect errors made while using a calculator.

Visual Check: Often errors of types 1, 2, 4, and 6 can be detected by a visual check. Look at the number you are keying into a calculator. Is the number displayed the number you intended to key? Look at the answer you have copied from the calculator display. Read the display again, to see if you copied correctly.

Not all errors of types 1, 2, 4, and 6 can be detected by a visual check. For example, a slight twist of the calculator may cause you to depress the $\boxed{\times}$ key when you actually intended to press the $\boxed{+}$ key. The visual display of most non-printing calculators shows numbers but not operations. Thus, you cannot look at the calculator display to see what operation key was depressed.

Do It Twice: A good way to check a calculation is to do it over again in a different order if possible. Thus, a column of numbers can be added from top to bottom and then from bottom to top. The product of two numbers can also be calculated in two different orders.

A subtraction can be done in either order. Thus, 726 − 329 is the same as −329 + 738. But, one must use care to avoid making an error in using this method to check an answer. For example, a student keys [7] [3] [8] [−] [3] [2] [9] [=] and copies down the displayed answer of 409. The student then continues by keying [−] [3] [2] [9] [+] [7] [3] [8] [=], expecting to get 409 again. However, the student actually gets 818. What went wrong? The student failed to clear the calculator between calculations! Thus, the second answer is actually 409 − 329 + 738, or twice the correct answer.

Finally, note that division cannot be done in a different order. But, one can check a division by doing the entire calculation over again, or the calculation can be checked by multiplication. Suppose we calculate that 7,182 ÷ 38 = 189. Without clearing the machine we can key in [×] [3] [8] [=] and expect to get 7,182 back again.

Such a check may not come out exactly, due to peculiarities of calculator arithmetic. On a typical eight-digit calculator we find 10 ÷ 3 = 3.3333333. When we multiply this by 3 the result is 9.9999999. We will discuss the peculiarities of calculator arithmetic more in Chapter 4.

Use Mental Arithmetic: The ready availability of calculators tends to increase the need and value of being good at mental arithmetic. One needs mental arithmetic to help catch errors made while using a calculator!

Suppose, for example, you need to calculate 3,794 − (87 × 16). It is "evident" that the answer should be considerably less than 3,794. Thus, it is easy to detect the error of keying in [3] [7] [9] [4] [−] [8] [7] [×] [1] [6] [=] which leads to 59,312 on most calculators.

Suppose you are faced with the following calculations:

a. $67\overline{)59{,}831}$ b. $59{,}831\overline{)67}$

Each calculation involves the numbers 67 and 59,831, and the ÷ operation. Thus, it is easy to key in one problem when you intend to key in the other. But, the answer to the first is obviously much larger than 1, while the answer to the second is obviously much smaller than 1. Thus, simple mental arithmetic detects the error of keying in wrong order.

Suppose you want to calculate 849 × 375. A common keying error is to depress the wrong operation key. But, it is easy to see that 849 ÷ 375, 849 − 375, and 849 + 375 all result in answers that are much too small.

None of the three methods of error detection is perfect. However, taken together they will detect most errors. You should practice using these methods whenever you use a calculator. Eventually you will find that they require very little extra effort, and that they do contribute significantly to your getting right answers.

Exercise Set 2.4

1. Using a calculator, do the following calculations as rapidly as possible. Do not spend time doing visual, mental, or other types of checking.

   a.   394   b.   89.67   c. $7.4\overline{\smash{)}89.6}$ d. $43.6 + (8.5 \times 4.7)$
       6,287 $\times\ 32.5$
        465
       9,875
      + 3,458

   Next do the calculations over again, taking your time to perform visual, mental and do-it-twice checks. Discuss your findings.

2. Examine the following calculations which have been performed on a calculator. Notice that none of the answers are correct. First, using your calculator, find the correct answers. Then specifically identify the most likely sources of errors in the problems (keying error, order-of-operations error, etc.). And, finally, state the types of check (visual, mental, do it twice) which would detect the errors involved.

   a. $362 \div 4 = 1,448$ e. $8 \div 6 = 0.75$
   b. $49 + 92 = 186$ f. $440 \times 86 = 3,440$
   c. $8,220 - 46 = 7,754$ g. $112 \div 11 = 11$
   d. $10 + 75 \div 5 = 17$

3. Being able to estimate the relative size of answers is an important skill in operating a calculator effectively. Without performing the indicated operations, mentally estimate the answers to the following problems and rank them from the largest to smallest. Then check your work with a calculator.

   a. $1,086 + 100 - 1,140$ e. $31 \times 42 - 649$
   b. 23.4×20.4 f. $12^2 - 74 \div 52$
   c. $4.6 \div 2.1 + 5.6$ g. $50 + 100 \times 2.1$
   d. $97 - 136 \div 1.36$

4. Time yourself as you use a calculator to calculate $1 + 2 + 3 \ldots +$ $98 + 99 + 100$. Time yourself again as you do the calculation in reverse order. Then observe that

$$1 + 100 = 101$$
$$2 + 99 = 101$$
$$3 + 98 = 101$$
$$\ldots$$

There are 50 pairs, each summing to 101. One can mentally, or by use of a calculator, see the correct sum is 5,050. Discuss what you learned by doing this exercise.

5. Paper-and-pencil competency tests in arithmetic computation often have the "passing" level set at 70% to 80%. Discuss the value or merit in mastering paper-and-pencil arithmetic at the 80% accuracy level. (Would you hire an 80% accuracy level person to do arithmetic for you?) Suppose students are allowed to use calculators. Decide upon an appropriate "passing" percentage for a competency test in this case, and support your answer by an appropriate discussion.

6. Suppose you are to present a lesson to a group of sixth-grade students on errors and their detection when using a calculator. Write a set of objectives, list a few activities, and give some suggestions for evaluating this lesson.

7. Select a grade level. In a brief report summarize the essential estimation skills students should possess at this level in order to effectively use a calculator.

8. Give some arguments to support the position that all students should be expected to memorize the 1-digit addition and multiplication facts.

THREE
Problem Solving: Understanding Problems and Processes

Of all creatures on earth, human beings have the greatest ability to create and solve problems. Roughly speaking, a problem is a situation in which there is a difference between how things are and how one would like them to be. Problems come in all sizes and in many different forms. We have war when we would like to have peace. We have poverty in an affluent society. We have some students who cannot read entering high school. We have environmental pollution and a shortage of energy.

Problem solving is a unifying theme in education. That is, much of education is directed toward understanding problems and learning how to solve them. Every academic discipline has its own types of problems, although often various disciplines overlap. Art, music, and poetry are concerned with the problem of expressing human feelings or emotions.

Mathematics provides a unifying theme in problem solving. Many of the problems of business, engineering, science, and the social sciences, can be represented and perhaps solved using mathematics. It is for this reason that mathematics is considered to be one of the "basics" of education.

In this chapter you will study problem solving from the point of view of mathematics. You will also examine the role of calculators in mathematical problem solving.

3.1 Some Problem Examples

Recently, a group of seventh graders were given a lesson which exposed them to the ideas given above. At the end of the lesson, they were asked to give some examples of problems. Although they were encouraged to describe general problems and not to restrict themselves to mathematics, all the examples they gave were mathematical, such as the following:

85 + 29 + 37   64.7 ⌐1892.75 $\frac{67.9^3 - 32.7^4}{43.1^2}$

$\sqrt{142.8}$ $125.79
                                        6.27
                                       83.42
                                      762.94
                                        7.31

Not only were all of the problems these seventh-grade students gave mathematical, they were all computational. There were no examples from geometry, such as:

1. Find the area and perimeter of this rectangle.

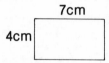

7cm

4cm

2. Name the figures given below.

a.   b.   c.   d.

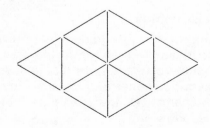

They gave no examples of puzzle problems, as given below:

1. Arrange six toothpicks to form four equal triangles.
2. Remove four of 16 toothpicks (as arranged in the figure below) so that four equal triangles remain. No toothpicks, which are not sides of a triangle, are to be left.

There were no "story" problems. That is, none of the examples required reading and figuring out what mathematical operations to perform, as in the following:

1. Donuts are $1.89 per dozen, but one gets a 15% discount on orders of five dozen or more placed a day in advance. You order twelve dozen donuts a day in advance. What is the total cost?

2. Mary buys four pounds of apples and six pounds of oranges for $3.30. If she had bought six pounds of apples and only four pounds of oranges she would have spent $3.70. What is the price per pound of each kind of fruit?

None of the students suggested any "proof" types of problems as follows:

1. Show that the sum of any two odd numbers is even, while the product of any two odd numbers is odd.

2. Suppose that you have a supply of dominoes and a checkerboard. Each domino is exactly the size of two squares on the checkerboard. It is easy to see how to cover the checkerboard with dominoes so that no dominoes overlap. Now suppose that two squares in diagonally opposite corners of the checkerboard are removed. Can the remaining board be covered with dominoes so that no two overlap? Prove your assertion.

Finally, none of the examples these seventh graders gave were examples of "real world" problems in which mathematics might be a useful tool, such as:

1. Determine an appropriate trajectory for a rocket that is to lift off from the earth, circle the moon, and return to earth.

2. In the United States approximately 50,000 people die each year in automobile accidents. The problem is to decrease this to less than 25,000. The last two examples are distinctively different from the others. It takes a considerable knowledge of physics and engineering to attack problem 1. Although problem 2 contains some numbers, it is not a mathematics problem.

A calculator is a useful aid in solving some types of problems, but it is not at all useful in solving other types. Keep this in mind as you work on the following exercises.

Exercise Set 3.1

1. Find the area and perimeter of the following rectangles.
   a. length = 7 cm, width = 4 cm
   b. length = 68.372 mm, width = 43.925 mm

   What is the same about solving these two problems? What is different?

2. Name the figures given below. Discuss the value, if any, of being able to name these figures.

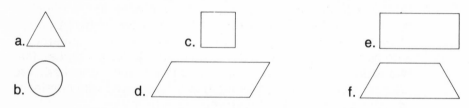

a.

b.

c.

d.

e.

f.

3. Solve the toothpick problems given in this section. Then give a written explanation of how you solved each problem.

4. Solve the donut problem given in this section. Then give a written explanation of how you solved the problem.

5. Solve the problem involving sums and products of odd numbers given in this section. A solution consists of a carefully written "proof," either using mathematical symbols or English words, which is as convincing to a sixth-grade student as it is to a college mathematics instructor.

6. Give several examples of problems from each of the following disciplines.
   a. Art or music
   b. History
   c. Political science
   d. Economics

   What features or general characteristics do these have in common?

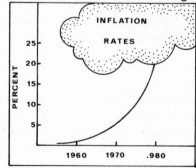

7. If you have a group of students at your disposal, perform the experiment reported in this section with them. Write a brief statement of your findings. How are your results similar to those reported in the seventh-grade experiment? How are they different?

8. What does the experiment reported in this section (and, the one you reported in Ex. 7) indicate about students' understanding of the term "problem?" In your estimation, why do students have this view of the meaning of a problem?

9. Make a list of general types of problems in which you think the typical adult makes use of a calculator.

3.2 What Is A Problem?

Definition of a Problem: A problem is said to exist when the following three conditions are satisfied:

1. **Given(s).** There exists a clearly defined *given*, or initial situation.

2. **Goal(s).** There exists a clearly defined *goal*, or final (desired) situation.

3. **Restrictions.** There exist clearly defined *restrictions* or guidelines as to what methods, activities, types of operations, etc. are allowed in moving from the given(s) to the goal(s).

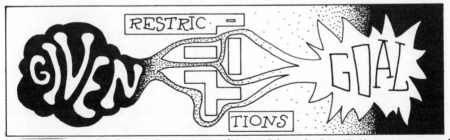

Often part of the statement of a problem is implicit, or assumed. For example, a teacher says, "find the sum of 17 and 13." Most likely, the teacher has in mind that the problem is to be done individually by each student, using paper and pencil or mentally. But, the restrictions are not stated. Some other options open to a student include: using a calculator, asking a parent, copying from a classmate, or counting on fingers and toes.

Problem Situations: Many of the things people call "problems" do not satisfy the formal, three-part, definition given previously. We will use the term *problem situation* to describe something which appears to have some of the characteristics of a problem. A major aspect of problem solving is working with problem situations to formulate clear-cut, well-defined problems. Determining the *givens, restrictions,* and *goals* is often the most difficult aspect of solving a real-world problem. Most mathematics books, including ones used in elementary and middle school classrooms, pay little attention to this difficulty.

Section 3.1 contained a number of sample problems. Actually, all of these were problem situations. As an example, consider the last problem, the traffic deaths situation. The initial situation (50,000 deaths per year) and the desired final situation (less than 25,000 deaths per year) are clear. But, what are the restrictions? Listed below are some possible (unrestricted) types of solutions.

1. Ban driving on all odd numbered days.
2. Install governors in all vehicles to restrict their speed to 40 km/hour.
3. Require all drivers to wear seat belts and shoulder straps, and require all vehicles to have air bags.
4. Limit the supply of fuel people can buy to four litres per person per day.

Any one of these might solve the problem. But, all have serious economic and political ramifications. What did the person who posed this problem situation have in mind?

Next, consider the following problem situation that might occur in a classroom. The teacher begins by presenting some examples:

$$\frac{4}{4} + 4 - 4 = 1 \qquad \frac{4}{4} + \frac{4}{4} = 2 \qquad \frac{4 + 4 + 4}{4} = 3 \qquad 4 + \frac{4 - 4}{4} = 4$$

The teacher then informs students that this is the four fours problem, the goal of which is to use exactly four fours at a time to produce as many of the integers in the range 1 to 100 as possible.

This is a problem situation, rather than a problem. The set of allowable operations is not clearly defined. For example, can multiplication be used?

$$4 \times 4 - \frac{4}{4} = 15$$

$$4 \times 4 + 4 - 4 = 16$$

$$4 \times 4 + \frac{4}{4} = 17$$

How about concatenation (i.e., using the 4's in whole number place value)?

$$\frac{44 - 4}{4} = 10 \qquad\qquad \frac{44 + 4}{4} = 12$$

Can parentheses be used?

$$(4 + 4) \times (4 + 4) = 64$$
$$4 \times (4 + 4) + 4 = 36$$

Now it may well be that the teacher is aware that the problem situation is not a well defined problem, and the intent is to force students to more carefully define the situation. But more likely, this subtlety is lost on the students, and a very good learning situation is seriously damaged.

Problem Solutions: We will conclude this section by looking at two more examples.

Find two positive odd integers whose sum is 17. You may use any aids to computation you wish, except that you must do your own work.

The problem has no solution! That is, a solution to the exercise is a carefully reasoned statement that the sum of two odd integers is always even, so the problem has no solution. *Many problems have no solutions!* One should not assume that merely because a problem can be carefully stated, it has a solution.

Find a whole number which, when multiplied by itself, gives 25. You may use any computational aids you wish, except that you must do your own work.

This problem has two solutions, $+5$ and -5. Many problems have more than one solution. It is important that students be aware of open-endedness aspects of problem solving.

Exercise Set 3.2

1. What part(s) are missing in each of the following "problems?"

a. 94.67
    43.68

b. 10.3cm

    6.2cm

c. I have a headache.

d. Taxes are too high.

e. There is too much unhappiness in the world.

2. The planet Earth has a population in excess of 4 billion, and the population is increasing at a rate of more than 80 million people per year. This helps create problem situations such as starvation, over crowding, and environmental pollution. Give a careful definition of one problem related to increasing world population. Make especially clear your restrictions upon solution methods. Do world leaders have to agree upon your restrictions, or some other set of restrictions, before progress can be made in solving the problem?

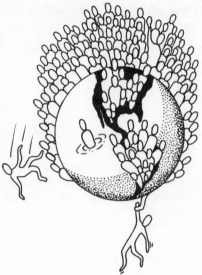

3. Examine several elementary school or junior high school mathematics textbooks. Look for a definition of "problem" and for a discussion of problem solving. Discuss your findings.

4. By use of a calculator, paper and pencil, or mental arithmetic find a positive whole number which when multiplied by itself gives 8,974. Identify the givens, restrictions, and goals in this problem. Then show (prove) that the problem does not have a solution.

5. State two different versions of the four fours problem given in this section, so that in each case the givens, restrictions, and goals are clearly defined.

6. Make up a problem that has exactly two solutions. Give a carefully reasoned argument (a proof) that your problem has the desired characteristic.

7. Make up a problem that has more than two solutions. How many solutions does your problem have? Prove your assertion.

8. Write a brief statement expressing why it is important to clearly define the givens, restrictions, and goals in problems given to elementary and middle school students.

3.3 Primitives

Think of some problems that are quite easy for you, problems you can solve quickly, accurately, and with little intellectual effort. We will call such problems *primitives*. Some primitives for you probably include counting by ones, tens, and hundreds; adding one-digit numbers; and recognizing certain geometric figures such as a triangle or a circle. It is evident that not all people have the same primitives. Also, your primitives vary over time as you learn new things and forget things you once knew.

The idea of a primitive is important for several reasons. First, primitives are usually problems that are worth solving in their own right. Second, they are building blocks, useful in solving more complicated problems. One must have one-digit multiplication as a primitive in order to acquire reasonable skill at paper-and-pencil multiplication (assuming the traditional algorithm for multiplication). More generally, it is common to solve big or complicated problems by breaking them into a sequence of smaller or simpler steps. It is desirable that the smaller steps be primitives.

Our educational system recognizes this idea. It tries to give all students a common core of primitives. This facilitates communication between teachers and students, and it provides a foundation for future studies.

Suppose that you have a calculator with a square root key, and you encounter a square root calculation problem. For you and your calculator the square root problem is a primitive! Supplying students with calculators, and providing instruction in their use, is a way of quickly increasing students' storehouse of calculational primitives.

The idea of primitives extends throughout mathematics, computer science, and all fields of human endeavor. Every discipline or activity has its "fundamentals" or "basics." These change as a field changes and also as the technology used in a field changes.

Exercise Set 3.3

1. While a primitive may be a single activity or task (2 + 2), it often is a category or general type of problem (being able to sum two one-digit positive integers). Make a list of the general types of mathematical problems that are primitives for you.

2. It is instructive to think of three general types of primitives.
   a. Memorized facts.
   b. Problems that can be solved by a brief mental effort, such as adding a one-digit number to a two-digit number.
   c. Problems requiring use of a tool, such as paper and pencil to add a short column of two-digit numbers.

   Assign each of your primitives from Ex. 1 to an appropriate category and discuss your conclusions.

3. Compare your list from the first exercise with another student's list or with the scope and sequence guide of an elementary or middle school mathematics textbook. List similarities and differences. What conclusions do you reach?

4. Select two disciplines or fields other than mathematics, such as art, music, science, basketball, knitting, etc. Make a list of the primitives for the disciplines you select. Discuss the relation between this and some aspects of mathematics education, and discuss the merits of your analogy.

3.4 Steps In Problem Solving

There are many different types of problems. We cannot give a simple plan that will solve all of them. But, there are certain general steps that are applicable to most mathematics problem-solving situations. Through learning these steps, you will improve your problem-solving skills. Also, you will gain better insight into the role of calculators in problem solving.

Many mathematics problems can be solved by following the five-step plan given below.

Five Steps to Problem Solving

1. **Understand** the problem. What are the givens, restrictions, and goals?
2. **Represent** quantities and ideas using appropriate mathematical notation.
3. **Plan** your method of attack. (Devise or acquire a solution plan.)
4. **Execute** (that is, carry out) the plan.
5. **Examine** the results for correctness and meaningfulness.

Story Problems: We will illustrate the five steps by solving the following problem:

A store sells bagels for $1.86 per dozen, but it gives an 8% discount on orders of ten dozen or more. What will it cost to buy eighteen dozen bagels at this store?

1. *Understand* The problem involves a situation in which one goes to a store and exchanges money for goods. Note that there is no bargaining over the price. You may never have seen or eaten a bagel, but this is not important to solving the problem. Finally, it is not necessary to know that a dozen means 12, but it is necessary to understand 8% and discount.

2. *Represent* The symbol $1.86 stands for, or represents, a certain amount of money. Similarly the symbol 18 represents a certain number of dozens of bagels, and .08 is a useful representation of 8%. It is often helpful to give names to the quantities to be worked with or determined. For example, we might use the following names:

Gross cost: cost before the discount
Discount: the amount of the discount
Net cost: gross cost minus discount

The named quantities, gross cost, discount, and net cost, are variables. That is, they are named quantities whose values may vary, depending upon the values other quantities are given in a particular problem.

3. *Plan* Our plan will be to calculate gross cost, discount, and net cost.
   a. Gross cost = $1.86 × 18
   b. Discount = .08 × (gross cost), with the result to be rounded to the nearest cent.
   c. Net cost = (gross cost) − discount

4. *Execute*
   a. $1.86 × 18 = $33.48 = gross cost
   b. .08 × $33.48 = $2.6784   This rounds to $2.68, the discount
   c. $33.48 − $2.68 = $30.80 = net cost

5. *Examine* We have produced a final answer of $30.80. Does this make sense? If the answer had come out $3,080 would you reject it out of hand, since this amount of money will feed an entire family for many months? Similarly, if the answer came out $3.08 would you detect this as being obviously too small?

   Some rough mental calculations may be helpful in examining an answer for possible correctness. If bagels were $2.00 per dozen and no discount were given, it is easy to calculate mentally that 18 × $2.00 = $36. The net cost should be less than $36, and it is.

   Similarly, even with the discount the bagels cost more than $1.50 per dozen. Can you calculate 18 × $1.50 mentally? If you think about 18 × 1.5, you can see the answer is $27. This should be less than the net cost, and it is. Mental calculations, such as these, help us to believe the answer we have determined makes sense and is likely correct.

In this problem arithmetic calculations occurred in two places: the execute and examine steps. Execution required accurate computation. A calculator may be useful in this step. In the examine step we used mental arithmetic. Generally speaking, mental arithmetic is often sufficient in steps 1, 2, 3, and 5. While a calculator is frequently useful in the execute step, depending on the complexity of the problem, it also may be helpful in steps 3 and 5 of the problem-solving process.

The bagel example was chosen because it illustrated all five steps of problem solving. How do textbook exercises such as the following fit in?

Computation Problems: Carry out the following calculations:

1. $6.94
    3.76
    .97
    + 2.43

2. 8,935
    × 62

3. $\dfrac{5}{12} + \dfrac{1}{3} =$

1. *Understand* It is evident that some thinking and previous training is needed to understand the problems. A typical first grader may not understand money and does not understand the notation used in problems 2 and 3.

2. *Represent* The represent step has been done for us; it is part of the given situation.

3. *Plan* For problems 1 and 2, the plan step merely consists of observing that these are standard addition and multiplication problems. We have memorized algorithms for them. For problem 3, we (mentally) decide to determine a common denominator, add, and simplify.

4. *Execute* The execute step is the main purpose of the set of exercises. The intent is to give the student practice in calculation.

5. *Examine* On each problem it is possible to estimate an answer, and thus to catch gross errors. For example, is $1,410 a reasonable answer for problem 1? Is the answer to problem 3 larger than 1 or less than ½?

Proofs: Next let us look at a "proof" type of problem from "higher" mathematics. Consider the following:

Show that the sum of any two positive odd integers is a positive even integer.

1. *Understand* To understand this problem one must understand words such as sum, positive, odd, even, and integer. Also, one must understand what it means to "show" and that the intent is to give a proof that works for every possible pair of positive odd integers. It is not sufficient to give an example, such as $3 + 7 = 10$, even though the addends (3 and 7) are positive odd integers and the sum (10) is a positive even integer. However, from this example we can conclude that we understand the problem.

2. *Represent* The represent and plan steps of problem solving are often closely intertwined. From basic definitions we know that a positive odd integer can always be represented in the form $2N + 1$, where N is a non negative integer. Thus, we decide upon the following representation:

Let $2C + 1$ be the first positive odd integer, where C is a non negative integer.

Let $2D + 1$ be the second positive odd integer, where D is a non negative integer.

Our choice of notation, 2C + 1 and 2D + 1, is based upon our previous mathematical training and insight into a possible plan.

3. *Plan* Our plan will be to add the two numbers, simplify the results, and try to show that the resulting quantity is a positive even integer.

4. *Execute* First number + second number = (2C + 1) + (2D + 1)

$$= 2C + 2D + 2$$
$$= 2(C + D + 1)$$

Since C and D are non negative integers, C + D + 1 is a positive integer. Thus, our final answer is, by definition, a positive even integer.

5. *Examine* Finally, we examine the overall process and results. Do they make sense? For example, could we use the same procedure to show that the sum of − 3 and − 1 is a positive even integer? Why not? Where does the proof breakdown? We know that 3 + 7 = 10 and 10 is a positive even integer. What are the values of C and D for this example? Does this make sense?

The odd numbers problem is typical of what one does in higher mathematics. It involves working with definitions and it involves some algebraic notation. The execute phase involves algebraic manipulation, and a calculator is of no value here. Overall, you should be aware that mental arithmetic is valuable at various stages of solving this problem. The understand, represent, plan, execute, and examine phases are each fairly difficult; each requires considerable understanding of mathematics.

Mathematics education in the elementary and middle school lays the foundation for students to eventually learn to deal with the more sophisticated mathematics problems arising at higher levels of education and in the real world. Students at these levels can learn to recognize and understand each of the five steps of problem solving. They can develop skill in applying these steps to problems which are suitable to their educational level. This process establishes a firm foundation for their future studies of mathematics and its applications.

Exercise Set 3.4

As you work exercises 1 through 16, identify the five steps of the general problem-solving plan you use to solve each problem. All of these exercises may be adapted easily for use with students.

1. Mary has six marbles and Terry has seven marbles. How many marbles do they have in total?

2. Apples are 3 kg for a dollar. How much will 4.6 kg cost?

3. Corn is a dollar per dozen ears. What will seven ears cost?

4. Jack purchases eight boxes of pencils at $3.24 per box, and a dozen reams of paper at $4.68 per ream. What is the total cost of Jack's purchases?

5. In Ex. 4 above there is a special sale. Pencils are discounted 16% and paper is discounted 24%. What is the total cost of Jack's purchases?

6. A number is multiplied by itself. The result, rounded to two decimal places is 7.45. Using a calculator, but not the square root key, find three different answers to this problem.

7. The sum of the measures of the interior angles in a triangle is 180°. What is the sum of the measures of the interior angles of each of the following.

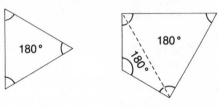

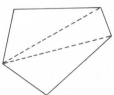

   a. Rectangle
   b. Quadrilateral
   c. Pentagon
   d. Hexagon
   e. A twenty-sided polygon

8. Jenny has nine U.S. coins. The total value of the coins is $1. How many of each type of coin (penny, nickel, dime, quarter, half dollar) does Jenny have? Find all possible solutions.

9. Prove that the sum of two positive even integers is a positive even integer.

10. Prove that the sum of an even integer and an odd integer is an odd integer.

11. Prove that the product of two even integers is an even integer.

12. Prove that the product of two odd integers is an odd integer.

13. Calculate and simplify.

   a. $\dfrac{1}{3} + \dfrac{5}{12}$

   c. $\dfrac{3}{4} - \dfrac{1}{3} + \dfrac{1}{12}$

   b. $\dfrac{1}{2} + \dfrac{1}{3} + \dfrac{1}{4}$

   d. $\dfrac{1}{2} + \dfrac{1}{4} - \dfrac{7}{12}$

14. A certain watch will run for exactly 100,000 seconds when it is fully wound. Suppose that the fully wound watch is started at 12:00 noon on a Monday. What time will it be, to the nearest second, when the watch stops? What day will it be, and will it be AM or PM?

15. Suppose that a certain clock will run for 100,000 minutes when fully wound. The clock is fully wound and starts running at 12:00 midnight on New Year's eve (that is, just as the New Year starts). If the year is not a leap year what will be the time (month, day, AM or PM, hour, minute) when the clock stops?

16. Solve Ex. 15 above for a 200,000 minute clock and for a 300,000 minute clock.

17. Make a list of the problems in this exercise set in which you used a calculator and the steps for which you used it. Write a short statement about how you found your calculator to be most useful.

18. If you have a group of students available, give them a brief lesson on the five steps to problem solving. Then, have them work several of the problems in this set. Compare your results with theirs.

19. Compare and contrast the applicability of the five-step problem-solving process to the solutions of the three types of problems discussed in this section (story problems, computation problems, and proofs).

20. After completing all exercises in this set, write a brief report which details the ways you have become a better problem solver.

3.5 Guess And Check

There are many general methods one might use in trying to solve a particular type of problem. Problem-solving skills can be improved by studying and practicing some of these methods. Guess and check, also called trial and error, is one of these general problem-solving methods. It is useful in a wide variety of problems and is often well-suited to use of a calculator. Although the examples considered here may be understood and performed best by middle school students, guess and check can also be used profitably by elementary students.

Suppose that you are asked to find a positive whole number which, when added to five times the square of itself, gives 1,462. You could solve the problem by systematic guessing and checking. The goal is to find a positive whole number n such that $5n^2 + n = 1{,}462$.

For n = 1	$5n^2 + n = 6$
For n = 2	$5n^2 + n = 22$
For n = 3	$5n^2 + n = 48$
For n = 4	$5n^2 + n = 84$
. . .	. . .
For n = 15	$5n^2 + n = 1{,}140$
For n = 16	$5n^2 + n = 1{,}296$
For n = 17	$5n^2 + n = 1{,}462$

From the last calculation we see that n = 17 is a solution to the problem.

A little thought suggests that we have done a lot of unnecessary work. Examine the following:

Guess n = 10	Calculate $5n^2 + n = 510$ Conclude n = 10 is too small.
Guess n = 20	Calculate $5n^2 + n = 2{,}020$ Conclude n = 20 is too large.
Guess n = 15	Calculate $5n^2 + n = 1{,}140$ Conclude n = 15 is too small.
Guess n = 17	Calculate $5n^2 + n = 1{,}462$ Conclude n = 17 is an answer.

In this sequence of guesses we quickly bracket an answer, and then systematically narrow down on it. This type of systematic guess and check can solve many different problems. It involves a combination of thinking with quite a bit of calculation. Often a calculator is a useful tool.

As a second example, suppose you are asked to find the cube root of 19 correct to two decimal places. That is, find n correct to two decimal places such that $n^3 = 19$. Systematic guess and check might proceed as follows.

Guess #	Value of guess n	n³	Conclusion
1	2	8	Too small
2	3	27	Too large
3	2.5	15.625	Too small
4	2.7	19.683	Too large
5	2.6	17.576	Too small
6	2.65	18.609625	Too small
7	2.67	19.034163	Too large
8	2.66	18.821096	Too small

From this table we conclude that the exact cube root of 19 lies between 2.66 and 2.67. Which should we select as our answer?

$$2.66^3 - 19 = 18.821096 = -.178904$$

$$2.67^3 - 19 = 19.034163 = .034163$$

If we examine the absolute value of the differences, we see $| 2.66^3 - 19| = .178904$, while $| 2.67^3 - 19 | = .034163$. We conclude that 2.67 is the desired answer.

Exercise Set 3.5

Use guess and check to solve exercises 1 through 7. Show your work in detail.

1. Find a positive integer which, when subtracted from three times its own square, gives 1,564.

2. Find a positive integer which, when multiplied by the next larger positive integer, gives 6,806.

3. Find the smallest positive integer whose square is a six digit number.

4. Find the largest positive integer whose square is less than eight digits in length.

5. Use systematic trial and error to find each of the following to two decimal place accuracy.

   a. $\sqrt{7}$ b. $\sqrt{169}$ c. $\sqrt[3]{13}$ d. $\sqrt[3]{216}$

6. Consider the function $f(n) = n^2 - 11n + 25$.
   By systematic guess and check, prove that there is no integer n, such that $f(n) = 0$. That is, show that the equation $f(n) = 0$ does not have an integer for a solution. Then, find two different solutions to the equation, each correct to two decimal places.

7. Solve the following equations to two decimal place accuracy.
   a. $n^2 - 15n + 32 = 0$

   b. $n^2 - 45 = 0$

   c. $n^3 - 17 = 0$

8. Make a list of the problems in this exercise set in which you used a calculator and the steps for which you used it. Write a short statement about how you found your calculator to be most useful.

9. Guess and check involves other problem-solving processes. Name several of them.

10. It has been said that guess and check is probably the least used process for solving problems in elementary and middle school mathematics classrooms. Why might this be the case? How will the use of the calculator affect this situation?

11. Name several topics within the elementary and middle school mathematics curriculum for which guess-and-check procedures may be useful.

FOUR
Formulas, Functions, and Calculator Arithmetic

In Chapter 3 you studied the five major steps for solving problems. You learned that if you encounter a problem that is quite different from anything you have seen before, accomplishing each step may be a major task. Appropriate training and experience can help you to perform these tasks.

PROBLEM SOLVING
1. Understand
2. Represent
3. Plan
4. Execute
5. Examine

There are certain types of problems which occur frequently, and the study of them is included in the school curriculum. For example, consider the 8.6 meter by 10.4 metre rectangle pictured. What is its area? The area-of-a-rectangle problem is considered important enough to be included in all students' educational programs. Most likely, you think to yourself: "Area is length times width." You may remember this piece of information in a more concise form as the formula A = lw.

8.6 m
10.4 m

The formula A = lw is a concise shorthand representation for steps 2 and 3 of solving the area-of-a-rectangle problem. It represents the key variables.

A = area of rectangle
l = length of rectangle
w = width of rectangle

It also contains the plan to solve the problem: multiply the length times the width. Of course, you must understand that l and w must both be given using the same unit of measure if the answer is to make sense.

Mathematical formulas are a very important part of mathematics. Each formula is a shorthand representation for steps 2 and 3 in solving a particular type of problem. A calculator is a very useful aid in the execute step of solving most such problems. Thus, the study of formulas is an important aspect of a calculator course. Two other closely related topics also covered in this chapter are the idea of a function and calculator arithmetic. But, first let us turn to a discussion of variables.

4.1 Variables

A variable is a quantity that has a name and whose value may change, depending upon the problem under consideration. A formula is a mathematical statement of equality involving variables and constants. For example, consider the familiar situation of traveling at a certain rate for a certain period of time. How far do you go? The answer is provided by the formula:

Distance = Rate × Time

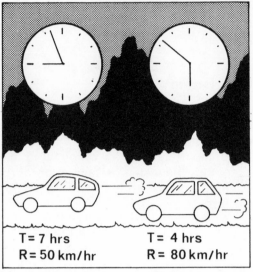

T = 7 hrs   T = 4 hrs
R = 50 km/hr   R = 80 km/hr

In this formula there are three quantities which have names and whose values depend upon the particular problem: distance, rate, and time.

Computer scientists like to give variables names which clearly specify their meaning. Thus, a computer scientist might use names such as:

YEARLY-INTEREST
HOURS-WORKED
RATE-OF-PAY
TAKE-HOME-PAY
DISTANCE-TRAVELED

The use of hyphens in these long variable names is merely to help the reader know each is a single unit, a single variable.

Mathematicians, on the other hand, like to use very short abbreviations for names of variables. They feel that it takes too much time, effort, and space to continually write out names such as distance, rate, and time. Thus, they like to use single letter abbreviations such as D, R, and T. In the formula D = RT they even leave out the multiplication symbol between R and T; it is assumed the reader understands that RT means R times T.

For another example, consider the problem of finding the perimeter of a rectangle. The formula is:

P = 2l + 2w

Here, P, l, and w are variables

while the number 2 is a constant. In this formula, the number 2 remains the same no matter what the values of l and w are in a particular problem.

Exercise Set 4.1

Each of the following problems can be solved by use of a common formula which you are likely to know, or can look up in a reference book. In each problem write down the formula(s) you use, specify the meaning of each variable (l = length, D = distance, i = interest, etc.), and solve the problem. Use your calculator if you wish. Note that Appendix A contains a brief discussion of the metric system.

METRIC

1 km

1. Find the area and perimeter of a rectangle with length 7.2 km and width 3.4 km.

2. Find the area and perimeter of a square with side length of 12.7 mm.

3. A person walks at the rate of 5.3 km/hour for 3.5 hours. What is the distance traveled?

4. A person walks 14.6 km in 4 hours. What is the average rate of walking?

5. A person deposits $75 in a bank that pays 5.5% simple interest per year. What will a year's interest be?

6. Eggs are 85¢ per dozen. What will five dozen eggs cost?

7. How many inches are there in 17 feet?

8. How many seconds are there in three days?

9. The sales tax is 6.5%, with amounts rounded upward to the nearest cent. What is the selling price for an item that lists at $47.50 before the sales tax?

10. Find the area of a triangle which has a height of 7.5 cm and a base of 8.4 cm.

11. A car travels 546 kilometres on a tankful of gas. If the tank holds 54 litres, what is the average kilometres per litre?

12. A circle has a radius of 10 cm. Find its circumference and area.

13. A car tire has a radius of 32 cm. How far will it go in 1 revolution? How many revolutions will it take to go 1 km?

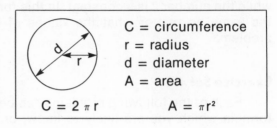

C = circumference
r = radius
d = diameter
A = area

$C = 2\pi r$ $A = \pi r^2$

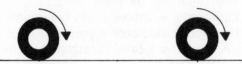

Suppose the tire is inflated to a higher pressure and its radius increases to 33 cm. Now how many revolutions will it make per km?

14. A wading pool is shaped like a rectangular box, with dimensions 3m by 2m by .5m deep. The pool is being filled by a garden hose that delivers 1,500 litres per hour. How deep will the pool be filled in 15 minutes?

15. On which of the above problems did you use your calculator? Could you have worked some of these problems either by paper and pencil or mental arithmetic as quickly and reliably as with a calculator?

16. Assisted by your answers to Ex. 15, write a brief statement about the nature of problems involving simple formulas and the necessity of a calculator to help solve them. Relate your comments to applications commonly found in the elementary or middle school classroom.

17. List other formulas you know that are part of the elementary or middle school mathematics program. Specify the meaning of each variable. For which of these formulas is a calculator well suited?

4.2 Understanding A Formula

What does it mean to "know" or understand a formula? It means more than merely having memorized the formula. Consider the Pythagorean Theorem, named after a famous Greek mathematician of the sixth century B.C.

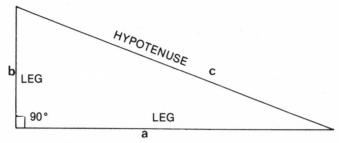

The formula itself is easy enough to remember: $a^2 + b^2 = c^2$. The problem situation referred to is that of a right triangle (that is, a triangle with a 90° angle). The hypotenuse of a right triangle is the side opposite the 90° angle. In the notation of the formula, its length is named c. The two sides which form the right angle are called legs; in the notation of the formula their lengths are named a and b. Thus, the formula states: (length of one leg)^2 + (length of other leg)^2 = (length of hypotenuse)^2.

The Pythagorean formula is useful in problems involving right triangles in which the lengths of two sides are known and the length of a third side is to be determined.

To find the length of the hypotenuse,

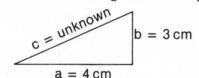

begin by matching the known parts of the triangle with corresponding parts of the formula. Then, solve for the variable whose value is unknown, as follows:

Given formula	$a^2 + b^2 = c^2$
Rearrange formula so the unknown is all by itself on left side.	$c^2 = a^2 + b^2$
Substitute in known values	$c^2 = 4^2 + 3^2$
Simplify and solve	$c^2 = 16 + 9$
	$c^2 = 25$
	$c = 5$

Used in this manner, the formula and some computation gives us a number, c = 5. By inspecting the units in the problem we conclude that 5 cm is the length of the hypotenuse. Does this make sense? It is longer than either of the other two sides, but not as long as their sum. Explain why this helps us to know the answer makes sense.

Next consider the following example:

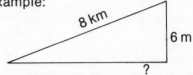

Figures used to specify problems are often not drawn to scale. Notice that the hypotenuse is 8 km in length, which is more than a thousand times the length of the known leg.

A typical error in solving the problem is to incorrectly handle the units. For example, one might proceed as follows:

Given formula	$c^2 = a^2 + b^2$
Identify known values	$c = 8$
	$b = 6$
	$a = ?$
Solve in usual manner	$a^2 = c^2 - b^2$
	$a^2 = 8^2 - 6^2$
	$a^2 = 28$
	$a = \sqrt{28}$
	$a = 5.29$ approximately

The (unthinking) problem solver produces the number 5.29 and then comes to put units on this number. Perhaps the conclusion is the unknown leg has the length of 5.29 km. This is obviously incorrect, since we know the sum of the lengths of the two legs must exceed the length of the hypotenuse.

The error is more apt to be detected if we carry along the units, as in the following:

$$c^2 = a^2 + b^2$$

$c = 8 \text{ km}$
$b = 6 \text{ m}$ ⎫
$a = ?$ ⎬ Here we might notice km versus m.
⎭

$a^2 = c^2 - b^2$

$a^2 = (8 \text{ km})^2 - (6 \text{ m})^2$

$a^2 = 64 \text{ km}^2 - 36 \text{ m}^2$

$a^2 = ??$ Here we surely notice that we need to have
a common unit of measure.

We leave it as an exercise for you to make use of the fact that 6 m = .006 km or that 8 km = 8,000 m and to solve the problem correctly. Note that a calculator is a useful tool in calculating the needed square root.

Exercise Set 4.2

Each of the following problems can be solved by using either a common formula or one provided in the problem. As you solve each problem, write down the formula(s), specify the variable(s), and be sure to keep track of the units of measure. Have your calculator handy, and use it as needed. Note that although many of the problems in this set contain quite sophisticated scientific concepts, they can be solved by most upper elementary and middle school mathematics students.

1. Find the area and perimeter of a rectangle which has a length of 6.4 km and a width of 7.8 m.

2. A right triangle has one leg of length 42 km and the other leg of of length 174 m. Find the area of the triangle and the length of its hypotenuse.

3. Suppose that concrete costs $145 for a cubic metre. What will the cost of the concrete be in a patio that is 4.5 metres long, 3 metres wide, and 9 cm thick?

4. The price of lumber is often quoted as dollars per thousand board feet, where a board foot is 144 in.^{3} Suppose that a particular grade of lumber is selling for $405 per thousand board feet. What will the cost be for a piece that is eight feet long, four feet wide, and a half inch thick?

5. The formula $C = 5(F - 32)/9$ relates temperature on the Celsius and Fahrenheit scales. What Celsius temperature corresponds to a Fahrenheit temperature of 68°? What Fahrenheit temperature corresponds to a Celsius temperature of 37°?

6. A ladder which is eight metres in length is placed so its base is two metres from the side of a building and its top is leaning against the building. If the building and ladder are on level ground how high up on the building does the ladder reach?

7. The formula $D = 4.9t^2$ gives the distance D in metres that an object will fall in time t seconds, when falling near the earth's surface. It is assumed the object has little air resistance, such as a steel ball. Suppose a steel ball is dropped from the top of a 300 m high

building. How far will it fall in 1 second, 3 seconds, 6 seconds? How long will it take to reach the ground, to the nearest .1 second?

8. The formula $V = 4.4 \sqrt{d}$ gives the velocity in metres per second for an object that falls a distance of d metres, subject to the same conditions as in problem 7. Find the velocity of the steel ball in Ex. 7 after 1 second, 3 seconds, 6 seconds, and as it impacts the ground.

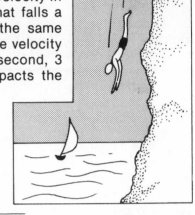

9. A diver dives from the cliffs of Acupulco, Mexico, a height of about 40 metres. Calculate how long the diver will be airborn and the impact velocity, assuming the formulas of Ex. 7 and 8 are valid.

10. The formula

$$D = \sqrt{1.5\,h}$$

gives the distance (in miles) to the horizon. The h in the formula is the height in feet. A person is standing at sea level, with his eyes exactly five feet above the ground. How far away is the horizon from him?

11. A person is looking out the window of an airplane flying at 34,000 feet. It is a clear day and she can see the horizon far away. How far away from the plane is the horizon?

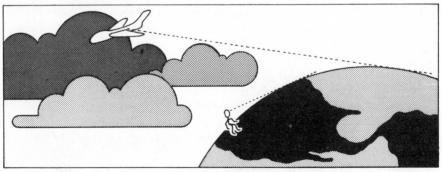

12. There is a similar formula using metric measurements, where h is in centimetres and the distance is in kilometres.

$$D = \sqrt{.126\,h}$$

The eyes of the person in Ex. 10 above are 152.4 cm above sea level. Find the km distance of the horizon.

13. Terry is standing on a mountain that rises, 2,540 metres above ground level. Given a clear day, how far away can she see?

14. For which of the above problems did you find your calculator to be a useful aid to problem solving? What aspects of solving these problems are best served by the calculator?

15. Comment on the nature of the formulas used in this section, the numbers involved, and the applicability of the calculator. Relate your remarks to the elementary or middle school classroom.

16. Several of the problems in this set deal with rather advanced scientific ideas. Do you see any danger in allowing students to use calculators for the purpose of solving problems which contain scientific or mathematical concepts they may not fully understand? Defend your answer.

4.3 Functions

A typical five-function calculator has function keys labeled $\boxed{+}$, $\boxed{-}$, $\boxed{\times}$, $\boxed{\div}$, and $\boxed{\sqrt{}}$. In this case the word *function* means an operation — a type of calculation — the calculator is constructed to perform. The idea of function is one of the most important ideas in mathematics. Some calculators have dozens of different function keys.

A calculator function may be thought of as a precise rule which takes as input one or more numbers and produces as output a number.

$$\left.\begin{array}{l}\text{input value}\\\text{or values}\end{array}\right\}\xrightarrow[\text{Rule}]{\text{Function}}\text{output value}$$

Each of the five functions of a five-function calculator can be understood by these diagrams.

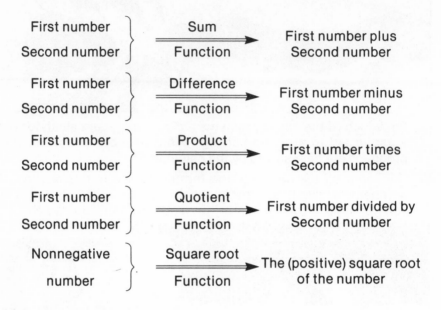

Some commonly used functions have names and special notation for their representation. Sum, difference, product, quotient, and square root are examples. Mathematicians have also developed ways of writing functions, called functional notation, that can be used for less familiar functions. For example:

$$f(x) = x^2$$

In this notation the "name" of the function is f. Listed after the name, in parentheses, are name(s) for the input value(s). After the = sign comes a mathematical expression stating how to calculate a value for the function.

Another name for the function $f(x) = x^2$ is the square function. Input is any number, while output is the square of the number. Thus, $f(5) = 25$, $f(6.2) = 38.44$, and $f(-4) = 16$. Some calculators have a key labeled x^2. This means that the calculator is constructed to automatically calculate values for the square function.

As another example, consider the function $p(x,y) = x^y$, In this function the number x is raised to the y power. We have named this function p to suggest the word "power." The function requires two input values. For example:

$$p\,(5,2) = 5^2 = 25$$
$$p(6,3) = 6^3 = 216$$
$$p(25,.5) = 25^{.5} = 5$$

(Raising a number to the .5 power means the same thing as taking its square root.)

As you can see, the power function is quite versatile. Thus, one is likely to find a key labeled x^y or y^x on most calculators with more than a half dozen function keys.

Exercise Set 4.3

Several of the exercises below may be used with elementary and middle school students. However, for the most part, the purpose of the set is to give you experience with the concept of function and its relationship to the calculator.

1. Explain the meaning of and give the common name for the following functions.
   a. $f(x,y) = x + y$
   b. $g(x,y) = x - y$
   c. $f(x,y) = xy$ Here the notation xy means x times y.
   d. $g(x,y) = x/y$

2. Suppose that a calculator has a key labeled $\boxed{\sqrt{}}$ or $\boxed{\sqrt{}\ x}$. What do you expect the output to be when this function is applied to:
   a.   25   b.   0   c.   −25
   Try these examples on at least two different brands of calculators and then discuss your conclusions. Note that you may experience some difficulty in entering a −25 into your calculator. Some calculators have a key labeled $\boxed{+/-}$, which is sign change function key. If one keys in 25 and then $\boxed{+/-}$, the result is a −25 in the calculator. On a simpler calculator, keying $\boxed{C}$ $\boxed{-}$ $\boxed{2}$ $\boxed{5}$ $\boxed{=}$ has the desired effect.

3. The reciprocal function is defined by $f(x) = 1/x$. A calculator key for it is generally labeled $\boxed{1/x}$. By calculator or other means find:
   a.   f(20)   b.   f(3)   c.   f(−3)   d.   f(0)

4. In Ex. 3 and 4 you encountered situations in which a function is not defined. In the real number system $\sqrt{-25}$ and 1/0 are not defined. This set of allowable input values for a function is called the

domain of the function. The domain of the recriprocal function is all nonzero numbers.

   a. What is the domain of the $\sqrt{}$ function?
   b. What is the domain for the $+$ function?
   c. What is the domain for the $\div$ function?

5. Many calculators have a function key labeled $\boxed{\%}$, called the percent function. There seems to be little agreement among calculator manufacturers as to the meaning of $\boxed{\%}$. Obtain a calculator with a $\boxed{\%}$ key. By trial and error or by studying the calculator's manual, figure out what this key does. Then explain its meaning and use.

6. If a calculator has both $\boxed{x^2}$ and $\boxed{x^y}$ keys, then either function could be used to square a number. Explain why a calculator manufacturer might design a calculator having both of these function keys. If you have access to such a calculator, try it out to see if both functions produce exactly the same values in a variety of calculations of squares of numbers.

7. The formulas $A = \pi r^2$ and $C = 2 \pi r$ give the area A and the circumference C of a circle of radius r. Recall that π is a constant, the ratio of the circumference of a circle to its diameter. The value of π is approximately 3.1415927, figured to seven decimal places. Many calculators have a $\boxed{\pi}$ key. Depressing the $\boxed{\pi}$ key is the same as keying in a value of π to full-machine accuracy. (Full-machine accuracy on an *eight*-digit calculator gives an approximation of π to *eight* digits.) Find the area and circumference of the following circles to full-machine accuracy.

   a. r = 8.4 cm   c. r = 1.97 mm   e. r = 25,000 m
   b. r = 145 cm   d. r = 0.0043 cm   f. r = 3,978 m

8. Real-world mathematical applications frequently make use of the measurements. Although the value of π is often used to full-machine accuracy, answers figured to full-machine accuracy are not always useful. For example, if we measured the radius of a circle to the nearest 0.1 cm, we could not compute the measure of the circumference with confidence closer than 0.1 cm. Thus for V = 8.4 cm the calculated circumference should be rounded to the nearest 0.1 cm. Now, suppose each radius given in Ex. 7 was measured with the indicated degree of accuracy. Calculate the circumference for each, and give your answers to the degrees of accuracy indicated.

9. Comment on the importance of students being able to read calculator output (answers to problems) appropriately. That is, what difficulties might occur if guidelines for reading answers are not given as part of instruction in solving real-world problems?

10. One of the most useful aspects of a calculator in the mathematics classroom is the role it plays in motivating and facilitating concept formation. Suppose you are to present a lesson to a group of fifth graders. The purpose of the lesson is to introduce the mathematical idea of function. Write an outline (a lesson plan) which details the ways you would use calculators to assist you in presenting this lesson. Compare your plan with an outline written by a colleague.

4.4 Formulas and Functions*

Formula and function are closely related ideas. Consider the Pythagorean formula $a^2 + b^2 = c^2$. This can be rewritten into formulas for a, b, or c as follows:

$$a = \sqrt{c^2 - b^2} \qquad b = \sqrt{c^2 - a^2} \qquad c = \sqrt{a^2 + b^2}$$

In functional notation we would denote these by:

$$f(b,c) = \sqrt{c^2 - b^2} \qquad f(a,c) = \sqrt{c^2 - a^2} \qquad f(a,b) = \sqrt{a^2 + b^2}$$

In a similar manner, consider the formula $D = RT$ which relates distance, rate, and time. The formula can be written in three forms, corresponding to three functions.

Formula	Function
$D = RT$	$D(R,T) = RT$
$R = D/T$	$R(D,T) = D/T$
$T = D/R$	$T(D,R) = D/R$

Applications of these formulas are as follows:

Terry rides her bicycle 10 km per hour for 2 hrs. How far does she go? $D = R \times T$ $D = 10 \times 2$ $D = 20\ km$	Terry bicycles 30 km in 2 hours. What is her rate of speed? $R = D/T$ $R = 30/2$ $R = 15\ km/hr$	Terry bicycles 40 km at the rate of 8 km/hr. How long does it take? $T = D/R$ $T = 40/8$ $T = 5\ hrs$

---

*The material of this section is algebraic in nature and may be omitted without loss of continuity.

For well-known, commonly-used formulas, the formula notation seems more convenient and comfortable to use than the functional notation. In either case, one should understand that a formula or function expresses a mathematical relation of equality between some quantities. A formula or function allows one to determine how variables in the relation change with respect to each other.

Functional notation is more common and more useful as one begins to deal with problems of higher mathematics. For example, how do the perimeter and area of a square change if we triple the length of its side? In functional notations:

$$P(s) = 4s \qquad P = \text{perimeter}$$
$$A(s) = s^2 \qquad s = \text{length of side}$$
$$A = \text{area}$$

Thus, we can calculate using 3s in the place of s:

$$P(3s) = 4(3s) = 12s$$
$$A(3s) = (3s)^2 = 9s^2$$

Now we calculate the ratios:

$$P(3s)/P(s) = 12s/4s = 3$$
$$A(3s)/A(s) = 9s^2/s^2 = 9$$

This type of algebraic maniuplation proves that tripling the side of a square multiplies its perimeter by 3 and its area by 9.

Exercise Set 4.4

1. Write the formula for the perimeter of a rectangle in the variety of functional notation forms needed to show how each variable relates to the other variables.

2. Write the formula for the area of a rectangle in the variety of functional notation forms needed to show how each variable relates to the other variables.

3. The formula $C = 5(F - 32)/9$ relates temperatures on the Celsius and Fahrenheit scales. Express C as a function of F, and F as a function of C, using common functional notation.

4. Prove that if the length of the side of a square is doubled the perimeter is doubled and the area is multiplied by a factor of 4.

5. Prove that if the length of each side of a rectangle is doubled the perimeter is doubled and the area is multiplied by a factor of 4.

6. A formula for the volume of a cube, in terms of the length of an edge, is $V = e^3$. The surface area is given by $S = 6e^2$. Determine what happens to the volume and surface area of a cube when the length of its edge is doubled. Prove your assertions.
7. The area and circumference of a circle are given by formulas $A = \pi r^2$ and $C = 2\pi r$. Suppose that one doubles the radius of a circle. How are the area and circumference changed? Prove your assertion.

4.5 Calculator Arithmetic

Up to this point we have allowed you (mistakenly) to believe that the mathematical functions sum, difference, product, and quotient are the same as the calculator functions $\boxed{+}$, $\boxed{-}$, $\boxed{\times}$, and $\boxed{\div}$. Certainly they are closely related. But consider:

$$1 \div 3 = .3333333333 \ldots \text{(real arithmetic)}$$

The "..." part indicates the threes repeat indefinitely.

$\boxed{1}$ $\boxed{\div}$ $\boxed{3}$ $\boxed{=}$ 0.3333333 (eight-digit calculator arithmetic)

Since this number has no "...", it is considered to terminate after seven decimal places.

While the difference is small, in some cases it can be significant.

The discussion which follows is for the most common eight-digit pocket calculators.

The real number line extends from "minus infinity" to "plus infinity" with no gaps or holes. There is no smallest or largest number. Between any two different numbers is another number, indeed, infinitely many.

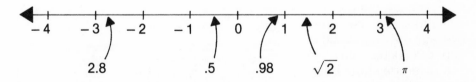

For a simple eight-digit calculator there is a smallest number, −99999999, and a largest number, 99999999. In between, the numbers are not equally spaced and there are only finitely many of them. For example, the next number larger than zero is 0.0000001. In the range between −10 and 10, the calculator number line consists of equally spaced points, with 0.0000001 being the difference between successive points.

At 10 and − 10, the spacing between points changes. Between − 10 and − 100 and between 10 and 100, the spacing between successive points is .000001. The spacing continues to change by a factor of 10 at each succeeding multiple of 10. Thus, between 1,000 and 10,000 the spacing is .0001 and between 1,000,000 and 10,000,000 the spacing is 0.1.

Suppose you are using an eight-digit calculator to solve a problem whose exact solution requires nine or more digits to represent. Eight-digit calculator arithmetic cannot produce and display the exact solution. This difficulty manifests itself in various ways. One way is in the checking of division calculations. On a calculator we find 30 ÷ 17 = 1.7647058. We multiply the answer by 17, expecting to get 30. Instead we get 29.999998.

An eight-digit calculator has, in its circuitry, the ability to calculate a sixteen-digit answer. (Recall that the product of two eight-digit numbers may be 16 digits in length.) The calculator uses this circuitry when doing an addition, subtraction, multiplication, or division. But, then it *truncates* (or rounds) the answer to eight digits. To truncate means to cut off (throw away) the extra digits.

The sixteen-digit circuitry insures that the commutative laws for addition and multiplication will hold. If A and B are (eight-digit or less) calculator numbers, then the sixteen-digit circuitry calculates the exact values for A + B or of A × B. These are the same as the exact values for B + A and B × A. Thus, when the calculator truncates (or rounds) to eight digits one gets an answer that does not depend upon the order in which the numbers were entered.

The calculator number line and calculator arithmetic can be conbined to produce some strange looking examples. For example, 99,999,999 ÷ 99,999,998 = 1.0 on an eight-digit calculator.

Use an eight-digit calculator to find the average of 6.0000001 and 6.0000003. Why is the average not between these two numbers, as one would expect in real arithmetic?

In real arithmetic we know that A × (B +

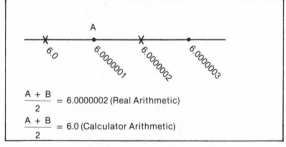

$$\frac{A + B}{2} = 6.0000002 \text{ (Real Arithmetic)}$$

$$\frac{A + B}{2} = 6.0 \text{ (Calculator Arithmetic)}$$

C) = A × B + A × C. This is the distributive rule for multiplication over addition. Use an eight-digit calculator to calculate the left side and the right side values for A = .5, B = 6.0000001, and C = 6.0000003. Do you get two different answers?

The real sum B + C is nine digits long. Thus, the calculator truncates (or rounds) it to eight digits, resulting in a truncation or rounding error in evaluating the left side of the equation. The calculator can perform the calculation on the right side exactly. (You will need to use paper and pencil or the calculator memory to record an intermediate result in doing this calculation.) Calculator memory is discussed in the next chapter.

Exercise Set 4.5

Exercises 1 through 12 given below are designed to emphasize features of arithmetic on an eight-digit pocket calculator that truncates answers to eight digits. All of these exercises may be adapted easily for classroom use with upper elementary and middle school students.

1. Mentally, and by use of a calculator, find:

   a. $\dfrac{3.0000001 + 3.0000005}{2}$ c. $\dfrac{6.0000001 + 6.0000005}{2}$

   b. $\dfrac{3.0000001 + 3.0000002}{2}$ d. $\dfrac{6.0000001 + 6.0000002}{2}$

   Discuss your findings and conclusions.

2. In the calculator number system there is a smallest positive number. What is it? What is the smallest positive number in the real number system? What is the result of dividing the smallest positive calculator number by 10 on a calculator?

3. Find the sum, using an eight-digit calculator, working from the top down and then from the bottom up. Explain why the results differ, and compare them with the exact answer.

$$
\begin{array}{r}
1{,}000.00000 \\
.00002 \\
.00003 \\
.00002 \\
.00001 \\
+ \quad .00002 \\
\hline
\end{array}
$$

4. State the commutative rule for multiplication of real numbers. Make up four relatively complicated multiplication problems. Use them to test the commutative rule for multiplication in calculator arithmetic. Discuss your findings.

5. 99,999,999 ÷ 99,999,998 is an example of two different numbers whose calculator quotient is exactly 1. Find two more examples of this sort.

6. Use your eight-digit calculator to calculate .008174 ÷ 928,365. The answer "should be" greater than zero. But an underflow occurs. That is, the machine answer is close enough to zero so that it truncates to zero. Make up two more division problems in which an underflow error occurs. The calculator user may detect this error by observing that an answer of zero occurs unexpectedly.

7. An overflow is an answer that is outside the calculator number line. On an eight-digit machine squaring 12,345 produces an overflow.

   An underflow error can occur in a multiplication, and an overflow error can occur in a division. Make up two examples of each of these situations.

8. Use a calculator with $\boxed{\sqrt{\ }}$ key to find $\sqrt{10}$. Square the answer. Next calculate $\sqrt{10}$ again, add .0000001 to the result, and then square this answer. Discuss your findings.

9. Observe that 12,345 = 1,234.5 × 10. Thus $(12,345)^2 = (1,234.5)^2 \times 100$. An eight-digit calculator can produce an approximate value for $(1,234.5)^2$ without producing an overflow. Use this calculation plus some mental arithmetic (multiplying by 100) to find an approximate value for $(12,345)^2$. Then use the same idea to find approximate values for the following.

   a. $(98,765)^2$ d. 379,462 × 847,935
   b. 82,943 × 61,748   e. 987,654,321 ÷ 84,932
   c. 629,374 × 6,847   f. 9,743,135,795 ÷ 689,427

10. The speed of light in a vacuum is approximately 186,282 miles per second. Using 365.25 as the number of days in a year, calculate an approximate value for a light year. This is the distance light travels in a year.

11. Does your calculator round or truncate? Write down details of a plan for testing a calculator to see if it rounds.

12. Devise a plan for finding the total of different numbers that can be displayed on your eight-digit calculator. Then, find the number of different numbers between 10 and 100, between 1,000 and 10,000, and between 100,000 and 1,000,000. Considering negative numbers as well, what is the total of different numbers your eight-digit calculator can display? Is this a finite number?

13. Listed below are several properties of the real number system:
    a. Commutative law of addition $a + b = b + a$
    b. Commutative law of $a \times b = b \times a$
        multiplication
    c. Associative law of addition $a + (b + c) = (a + b) + c$
    d. Associative law of $a \times (b \times c) = (a \times b) \times c$
        multiplication
    e. Distributive law $a \times (b + c) = a \times b + a \times c$
    f. Additive identity   Since $a + 0 = a$, 0 is the
                                       additive identity.
    g. Multiplicative identity   Since $a \times 1 = a$, 1 is the
                                       multiplicative identity.
    h. Additive inverse   Since $a + {}^{-}a = 0$, ${}^{-}a$ is the
                                       additive inverse of a.
    i. Multiplicative inverse   Since $a \times 1/a = 1$, 1/a is the
                                       multiplicative inverse of a,
                                       provided $a \neq 0$.

    Which of these are *not* properties of the calculator number
    system? Defend your answer.
14. Write a short report on the importance of developing an awareness
    of calculator arithmetic among students who use calculators in
    school mathematics. Illustrate your report by giving numerous
    examples.
15. Make a list of topics within the school mathematics curriculum
    that can be motivated and facilitated by various aspects of calcula-
    tor arithmetic. Then, select one of these topics at a particular grade
    level and write an outline (a lesson plan) which gives the ways you
    would use calculator arithmetic to assist you in presenting this
    lesson. If you have a group of students available, try the lesson
    with them. Discuss your results.

FIVE
Memory: The Calculator's Storehouse

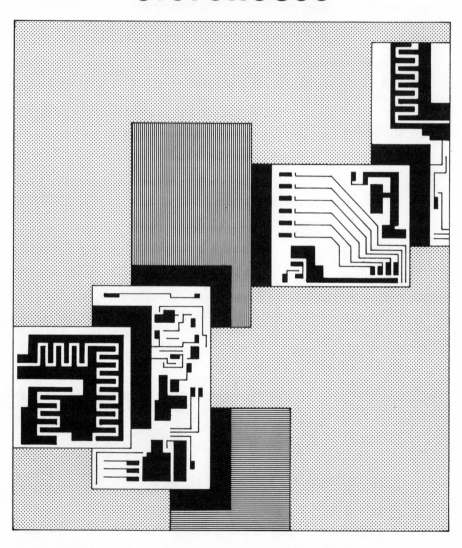

The word memory tends to suggest a human mind and higher-level functions of the brain. But, a calculator memory is merely storage space in which numbers and operations can be stored. There is nothing brain-like or human-intelligence-like in a calculator memory. It is just some electronic components and circuitry designed to operate in a specific fashion. In this chapter you will study calculator memory and some of its applications.

5.1 Machines With Memory

Every calculator has a memory where numbers and operations can be stored. A good analogy is a set of mail-boxes, each labeled with their owner's name. The content of a mailbox can change. In keeping with this analogy one should think of calculator memory as named storage spaces whose contents can be changed. Notice that this is almost the same as our definition of a variable.

What happens when we key 2 8 $+$ 3 9 $=$ into a calculator? We begin by pushing the 2 key. The number 2 is stored in a memory location and is displayed on the calculator's screen display. We continue by pushing the 8 key. Now 28 is stored in memory and displayed.

Next, we push the $+$ key. The calculator stores this operation in its memory; the display does not change. We continue by keying in 3 9, so that 39 is stored and displayed. Finally, we push the $=$ key. This instructs the calculator to carry out (execute) the stored operation + on the pair of stored numbers 28 and 39. The answer, 67, is stored in a memory location and displayed as output.

Some calculators have larger memories than others. This means they can store more numbers and operations. Consider the following calculation:

$$\overset{\textit{Part 1}}{(49.3 \times 84.7)} + \overset{\textit{Part 2}}{(81.6 \times 29.1)}$$

The least expensive pocket calculator can carry out the calculation of Part 1 or of Part 2. A calculator with more memory may be able to store the answer to Part 1 while it carries out the calculation of Part 2. This allows one to complete the entire calculation without writing down the answer to Part 1 and then keying it in to add to the answer to Part 2.

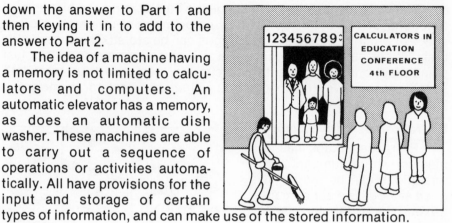

The idea of a machine having a memory is not limited to calculators and computers. An automatic elevator has a memory, as does an automatic dish washer. These machines are able to carry out a sequence of operations or activities automatically. All have provisions for the input and storage of certain types of information, and can make use of the stored information.

Exercise Set 5.1

1. Explain the operation of the [CE] and [C] keys in terms of their effects upon the contents of calculator memory.

2. Does a typical automatic elevator have buttons corresponding to the [CE] or [C] keys of a calculator? Discuss this situation.

3. Suppose you push the [+] key when you intend to push the [×] key. Immediately afterwards, before keying in the next number, you detect this error. Experiment with your calculator to see if, or how, the error is easily corrected. Explain your findings in terms of calculator memory.

4. On some calculators the keying sequence [5] [+] [4] [×] [8] [=] will produce the correct answer for the calculation 5 + (4 × 8). Explain why such a calculator must be able to store at least three numbers and two operations.

5. Make a list of common machines that have a memory. For each, discuss briefly the capabilities and limitations of the memory.

6. Some calculators maintain their memory contents when turned off. One application of this technology is in bank-book calculators. In these calculators a person's bank balance is permanently stored in a memory location. Give several additional useful applications of such technology.

7. The memory of a computer is much like the memory of a calculator, only considerably larger. Give an example of a problem that requires a large memory for its solution.

5.2 Simple Memory

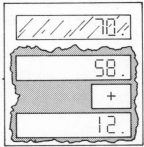

In this section you will study the memory of a simple four-function calculator in more detail. The goal is to understand how the contents of various memory locations change as a calculation is keyed in and executed. This understanding will lead to understanding of the automatic constant feature found in many calculators.

A simple four-function calculator has memory space to store a pair of numbers that are input to an operation such as $+$, $-$, $\times$, or $\div$. We will label these memory locations S_1 and S_2 to suggest storage location #1 and storage location #2. The calculator has an arithmetic register, a place where arithmetic is done. For an eight-digit calculator this space can store a sixteen-digit number. We will call it A. Finally, the calculator can store an operation, such as $+$, $-$, $\times$, or $\div$. We will designate this memory space by Op, short for operation.

We will use rectangular boxes to denote the memory locations.

S_1 [   ]   Op [   ]

S_2 [   ]   A [   ]

You should be aware that this model of a calculator is considerably simplified and idealized from the internal workings of an actual calculator. But, it is good enough to help you learn about how a calculator functions.

We will trace through what happens in each location as ③ ⑦ ☒ ④ ⑥ ␀ is keyed in. We begin by clearing the calculator.

Memory is cleared.

S_1 [0.   ]   Op [NONE   ]

S_2 [0.   ]   A [0.   ]

For a calculator with a screen display, the display mechanism always shows the contents of the S_1 storage location. Thus, initially, 0. is displayed. The calculator begins as ③ ⑦ is keyed in. It is stored in S_1 and, of course, displayed.

③ ⑦ is keyed and is displayed.

S_1	37.	Op	NONE
S_2	0.	A	0.

Next, the operation ⨉ is keyed. On almost all calculators this causes two things to happen. The operation × is stored in the Op location and a copy of the contents of S_1 is made and placed in S_2.

③ ⑦ ⨉ is keyed.

S_1	37.	Op	×
S_2	37.	A	0.

Next, ④ ⑥ is keyed. This goes into S_1, replacing its previous contents, and is also displayed.

③ ⑦ ⨉ ④ ⑥ is keyed.

S_1	46.	Op	×
S_2	37.	A	0.

Finally, the ⟍=⟋ key is pushed. This instructs the calculator to apply the operation stored in Op to the two numbers stored in S_1 and S_2. The arithmetic register A is used in this process. After the answer has been calculated into the A register, a truncated (or rounded, on some calculators) copy of it is placed into the S_1 register. Thus, the answer is displayed.

③ ⑦ ⨉ ④ ⑥ ⟍=⟋ is keyed. The calculation is completed and the answer is displayed.

S_1	1702.	Op	×
S_2	37.	A	1702.

Notice that upon completion of a calculation each memory location has some contents. The manufacturer of a calculator can design the machine to take advantage of this. What do you think will happen if 🔲= is keyed again? Most calculators have an automatic constant for multiplication. This means that pushing the 🔲= key will cause the calculator to carry out the multiplication 37 × 1,702 in this case.

$$\boxed{3}\ \boxed{7}\ \boxed{\times}\ \boxed{4}\ \boxed{6}\ \boxed{=}\ \boxed{=}\ \text{is keyed.}$$

S₁	62974.

Op	×

S₂	37.

A	62974.

The "automatic constant" is the first number keyed in, the 37. Several applications of the automatic constant, and related ideas, are illustrated in the following exercises.

Exercise Set 5.2

1. Show the contents of each memory location at each step of the calculation 14 ÷ 9 = .

2. What does your calculator give as the results of $\boxed{C}\ \boxed{3}\ \boxed{\times}\ \boxed{=}$? Most calculators give 9, the square of 3. Explain why, and give an example of a useful application of this automatic squaring feature.

3. Suppose you have just completed the calculation 1.12 × 8.45 = . What does your calculator give if you next key in $\boxed{6}\ \boxed{.}\ \boxed{3}\ \boxed{5}\ \boxed{=}$? Most calculators will give 7.112, which is 1.12 × 6.35. The first number, 1.12, is treated as an "automatic constant" for multiplication. Explain how this works in terms of calculator memory.

4. A particular store sells each item at 36% above the wholesale cost. Thus, the retail price is 1.36 times the wholesale price. Using the ideas of Ex. 3, find the retail price for each of the following wholesale prices. Round to the nearest cent.
   a. $89.70   c. $9.63
   b. $104.65   d. $37.82

5. Consider the following keying sequences. First push $\boxed{C}$.

   $$\boxed{4}\ \boxed{\times}\ \boxed{CE}\ \boxed{+}\ \boxed{6}\ \boxed{=}\qquad \boxed{4}\ \boxed{\times}\ \boxed{+}\ \boxed{6}\ \boxed{=}$$

   Think about what you would expect the answers to be, then try them on several different brands of calculators. Explain the results in terms of memory functioning.

6. Carry out the following calculations. Give your answers to full-machine accuracy.

   a. $2.71828^6 \times 83.7$
   b. $3.1415927^9 \times 2.47$
   c. 184.9×8.7394^5

7. What does your calculator produce for the following keying sequence?

Some calculators will produce 24, but most will produce 14. That is, they do not have an automatic constant for addition. Give an explanation of what this tells us about how calculator memory functions in this case.

8. Observe the output display of your calculator as you key the following:

$$\boxed{2}\ \boxed{+}\ \boxed{5}\ \boxed{+}\ \boxed{3}\ \boxed{+}\ \boxed{4}\ \boxed{-}\ \boxed{2}\ \boxed{=}$$

Notice that intermediate answers are displayed after the second and subsequent operation keys are depressed. Use this example to explain how the calculator memory system functions in this chain calculation.

9. Most calculators have an automatic constant for division. Discover and explain how this feature works. Note that such a calculator must have memory in addition to the S_1, S_2, and A we have discussed. Use it to solve the following problems.

   a. $16 \div 2 \div 2$
   b. $894.3 \div 16.75 \div 16.75 \div 16.75$
   c. $1{,}024 \div 2^{10}$

10. The formula for how money ac-
    cumulates when compound in-
    terest is added is:

    $A = p(1 + r)^t$

    r = interest rate per time period
    t = number of time periods
    p = initial principal
    A = final amount

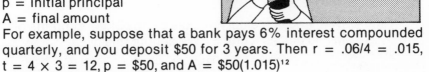

    For example, suppose that a bank pays 6% interest compounded
    quarterly, and you deposit $50 for 3 years. Then r = .06/4 = .015,
    t = 4 × 3 = 12, p = $50, and A = $50(1.015)^{12}
    a. Calculate the value of A above.
    b. What will the final amount of money be if the $50 is left in the
       bank for a total of eight years?
    c. Solve a and b above using an interest rate of 8% per year.
    d. Solve a, b, and c above assuming that money is compounded
       yearly rather than quarterly.

11. One of the early-model pocket calculators had a six-digit display,
    but claimed to be able to give twelve-digit accuracy. After a calcu-
    lation was completed, the six most significant digits of the answer
    were displayed. A special key was depressed to display the next six
    digits of the answer. Explain how this calculator works in terms of
    the memory box pictures used in this section.

5.3 Four-Key Memory

    The simple memory system we have just
covered is not adequate for many calculations.
For example:

$$(89.74 \times 63.75) + (18,219 \div 67.8)$$

An answer to the first part of the calculation
needs to be found and temporarily stored. Then
an answer to the second part is calculated, and
combined with the first. Temporary storage can
be done using paper and pencil. Alternatively, a
calculator can be constructed with an extra
memory location for the temporary storage of an
answer.

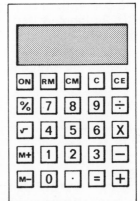

    A four key memory system calculator has
an "extra" memory location, which we will call M. This location, like S_1
and S_2, can store a number. The four calculator keys CM, RM, M+,
and M − operate as follows:

CM   The CM (clear memory) key places 0. into the
      memory location, M. We denote this by:

$$\text{CM} \quad 0. \longrightarrow M$$

The other three keys involve both M and S_1.

RM   RM (recall memory) makes a copy of the contents of
      M and places it into S_1. We denote this by:

$$\text{RM} \quad M \longrightarrow S_1$$

The contents of M remain unchanged in M.

M+   The M+ key adds S_1 to M and places the answer in
      M.

$$\text{M+} \quad M + S_1 \longrightarrow M$$

M−   The M− key subtracts S_1 from M and places the
      answer in M.

$$\text{M−} \quad M - S_1 \longrightarrow M$$

The contents of S_1 remain unchanged in S_1. (Note that the key labeled
CM is labeled MC on many calculators. Similarly, the key RM is
often labeled MR.)

   Use a calculator with a four-key memory system to follow along as
we solve the problem $(7 \times 9) - (36 \times 4)$.

Step 1:   Calculator is cleared by keying C and CM.

S_1	0.		M	0.
S_2	0.		Op	NONE
A	0.

Step 2:   The first part, $\boxed{7}$ $\boxed{\times}$ $\boxed{9}$, is keyed

S₁	9.	M	0.
S₂	7.	Op	×

A	0.

Step 3: $\boxed{=}$ is keyed to complete the first calculation.

S₁	63.	M	0.
S₂	7.	Op	×

A	63.

Step 4: $\boxed{M+}$ is keyed to get this intermediate answer into memory location M.

S₁	63.	M	63.
S₂	7.	Op	×

A	63.

Step 5:   The second part, $\boxed{3}$ $\boxed{6}$ $\boxed{\times}$ $\boxed{4}$, is keyed. Note that we can push $\boxed{C}$ before keying $\boxed{3}$ $\boxed{6}$ $\boxed{\times}$ $\boxed{4}$, but this is not necessary.

S₁	4.	M	63.
S₂	36.	Op	×

A	63.

Step 6: $\boxed{=}$ is keyed to complete the second calculation.

S₁	144.	M	63.
S₂	36.	Op	×

A	144.

Step 7: $\boxed{M-}$ is keyed to subtract this result from memory location M.

S₁	144.	M	− 81.
S₂	36.	Op	×
A	144.		

Step 8: $\boxed{RM}$ is keyed to display the contents of M, the desired answer.

S₁	− 81.	M	− 81.
S₂	36.	Op	×
A	− 81.		

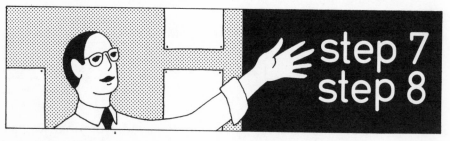

Exercise Set 5.3

1. Use a calculator with a four-key memory together with the eight-step example given in this section to solve the following:

   a. (6 × 8) + (12.9 × 4.2)
   b. (48.3 ÷ 1.4) − (86 × 4)

2. Work the problem, (7 × 9) − (36 × 4), illustrated in steps 1 through 8 above, but this time leave out steps 3 and 6. Write down what you learn from this experiment. (Note that most calculators will give the same final answer, − 81, when steps 3 and 6 are omitted.)

3. Show the contents of each memory location after each step in performing the following calculations making use of a four-key memory system.

$$\frac{9}{13} - \frac{3}{7}$$

4. Complete the following table, making use of calculator memory as seems appropriate.

Item	Quantity	Price each	Item Total
Eggs	17 dozen	$.87 per dozen	$14.79
Bread	24 loaves	$.53 per loaf	a. _____
Margarine	9 lbs.	$.64 per lb.	b. _____
Jam	8 jars	$1.34 per jar	c. _____
		Total for all items	d. _____

5. Calculate $1 + \dfrac{1}{2} + \dfrac{1}{3} + \ldots + \dfrac{1}{10}$

   Do it first working from left to right, and then do it working from right to left.

6. Perform the following calculations. (Do b only if your calculator has a $\sqrt{\ }$ key.)

   a. $\dfrac{\dfrac{5}{12} - \dfrac{3}{7}}{\dfrac{5}{16}}$

   b. $\dfrac{\sqrt{2} + \sqrt{3} + \sqrt{4}}{3}$

7. Mentally determine the contents of M after the following keying sequences. Check using a calculator.

   a. $\boxed{CM}$ $\boxed{C}$ $\boxed{5}$ $\boxed{M+}$ $\boxed{+}$ $\boxed{2}$ $\boxed{=}$

   b. $\boxed{CM}$ $\boxed{C}$ $\boxed{8}$ $\boxed{M+}$ $\boxed{\times}$ $\boxed{5}$ $\boxed{=}$ $\boxed{M-}$ $\boxed{RM}$

   c. $\boxed{CM}$ $\boxed{C}$ $\boxed{3}$ $\boxed{M+}$ $\boxed{M-}$ $\boxed{9}$ $\boxed{M+}$ $\boxed{M-}$

   d. $\boxed{CM}$ $\boxed{C}$ $\boxed{9}$ $\boxed{M-}$ $\boxed{\times}$ $\boxed{=}$ $\boxed{M+}$

   e. $\boxed{CM}$ $\boxed{C}$ $\boxed{3}$ $\boxed{M+}$ $\boxed{=}$ $\boxed{M+}$ $\boxed{=}$ $\boxed{M+}$

8. Carry out the following experiment.

   $\boxed{CM}$ $\boxed{C}$ $\boxed{1}$ $\boxed{2}$ $\boxed{M+}$ $\boxed{3}$ $\boxed{\div}$ $\boxed{RM}$ $\boxed{=}$

   The first five keystrokes put 12 into M. The remaining steps show how a number in M can be used as a divisor of a number in S_1. The answer is .25. Use this idea to solve the following problems without writing down intermediate answers.

   a. $\dfrac{8}{17 \div 41 + 9}$

   b. $\dfrac{62.4 \times 9.8 - 12.85}{184 \div 3.8 + 61.5}$

   c. $\dfrac{3974 \div 16.8 + 275.6}{38.5 \times 62.8 - 94.6 \div 13.5 + 84.3}$

9. Show the contents of each memory location after each keystroke in the following problems.
   a. $\boxed{\text{TURN ON}}$ $\boxed{6}$ $\boxed{\text{M}-}$ $\boxed{\times}$ $\boxed{5}$ $\boxed{=}$ $\boxed{\text{M}+}$ $\boxed{\text{RM}}$
   b. $\boxed{\text{TURN ON}}$ $\boxed{8}$ $\boxed{\text{M}+}$ $\boxed{\div}$ $\boxed{2}$ $\boxed{=}$ $\boxed{\div}$ $\boxed{\text{RM}}$ $\boxed{=}$

10. Solve the following problem using your calculator.

$$\frac{\dfrac{5}{7} - \dfrac{3}{13}}{\dfrac{11}{13} + \dfrac{5}{12}}$$

Use this example as a basis for a discussion of the desirability of adding still another memory location, say N, with keys $\boxed{\text{CN}}$ $\boxed{\text{RN}}$ $\boxed{\text{N}+}$ $\boxed{\text{N}-}$.

11. What would be the advantages and disadvantages of adding $\boxed{\text{M}^{\text{X}}}$ and $\boxed{\text{M}\div}$ keys to a four-key memory system calculator?

5.4 Calculator Functions

We have indicated that calculator circuitry is capable of performing operations such as $+$, $-$, $\times$, $\div$, and $\sqrt{}$. The circuitry does this by executing a detailed step-by-step set of directions, an algorithm, stored in memory. That is, a calculator has a considerable quantity of memory in addition to the S_1, S_2, A, Op, and M discussed so far in this chapter. The contents of these memory locations are set at the calculator factory and cannot be changed by the calculator user.

The detailed step-by-step sets of directions stored in a calculator memory are called *programs*, or calculator programs. They are designed by people called programmers who have detailed knowledge of the circuitry, and of the algorithms to be performed.

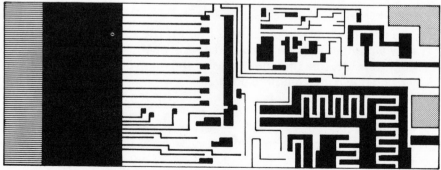

A calculator program for even a simple operation, such as +, is quite complicated. To understand and appreciate this, recall the details involved in lining up the decimal point and carrying out the digit-by-digit calculation of 6.94 + 83.7.

More complicated functions, such as $\sqrt{\ }$, are built up using the simpler (programmed in) functions of +, −, ×, and ÷. An algorithm for calculating $\sqrt{\ }$, known as Newton's method, is shown in the adjacent flowchart. (Flowcharts are discussed in the next section.) When you push the $\boxed{\sqrt{\ }}$ key of a calculator an algorithm

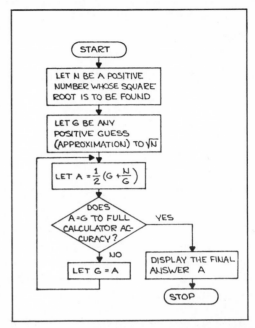

such as this, stored in the calculator's memory, is automatically carried out to produce the desired answer.

Newton's method is an averaging process. We will study an example to see how it works. Suppose we set N = 17 and use G = 4 as an initial guess to $\sqrt{17}$. Observe that $4 < \sqrt{17}$ and $\sqrt{17} < 17/4$. That is, the two numbers 4 and 17/4 bracket the desired answer $\sqrt{17}$.

$$\sqrt{17}$$

4   17/4

Newton's method computes the average of these two values (a value midway between them) as the next approximation to $\sqrt{17}$.

$$\sqrt{17}$$

4   ↑   17/4

New Guess $\frac{1}{2}(4 + \frac{17}{4})$

The averaging process is used over and over again. The two numbers G and N/G will always bracket the quantity $\sqrt{N}$. Mathematicians have proven that this process rapidly closes down on an answer no matter what the value of the initial guess G (provided only that it be positive).

If we let G_1 denote the initial guess, $G_1 = 4$ for the $\sqrt{17}$ problem, we get:

$G_1 = 4$

$G_2 = \frac{1}{2}(4 + \frac{17}{4}) = 4.125$

$G_3 = \frac{1}{2}(4.125 + \frac{17}{4.125}) = 4.123106$

$G_4 = \frac{1}{2}(4.123106 + \frac{17}{4.123106}) = 4.1231056$

$G_5 = \frac{1}{2}(4.1231056 + \frac{17}{4.1231056}) = 4.1231056$

These calculations were all done on an eight-digit calculator. Thus, we have calculated $\sqrt{17} = 4.1231056$ to eight-digit accuracy.

Details of how to make an accurate initial guess and exactly when to stop the algorithm are topics studied in *numerical analysis*, which is a branch of applied mathematics. The study of numerical analysis is usually based upon a good working knowledge of calculus. Thus, these details are well beyond the scope of this book.

Numerical analysts develop and study algorithms for solving a wide variety of mathematical problems. For example, how does the $\boxed{x^y}$ key actually work? A numerical analyst can supply the details. This knowledge can be embodied in calculator circuitry and memory. The calculation x^y then can easily become a primitive for a person who hasn't even heard of calculus, much less studied it in detail.

Exercise Set 5.4

1. Follow the Newton method flowchart, using a calculator, to complete the following table.

N	G	N/G	$A = \frac{1}{2}(G + N/G)$
9	1	9	5
9	5	1.8	
9			
9			
9			

2. For N and initial guess G_1 given below, calculate the next three guesses (approximations) G_2, G_3, G_4 in Newton's method.

   a. $N = 17, G_1 = 4$
   b. $N = 17, G_1 = 1$
   c. $N = 17, G_1 = 100$

3. Follow the Newton method flowchart for $N = 169$ with an initial guess $G = 13$. Explain what happens.

5.5 Flowcharts

In the last section we used a flowchart to represent Newton's method for calculating square roots. A flowchart is merely a set of directions in boxes, connected by arrows to help indicate the order in which the directions are to be executed. A flowchart is a useful method for representing a plan to solve a type of problem.

To make flowcharts easier to read people have agreed upon standard shapes for the boxes, and assigned meaning to different shapes. For example, the beginning and end(s) of a flowchart are indicated by elliptical boxes.

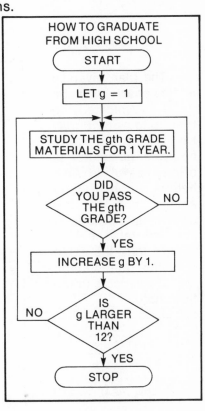

An action that is to be carried out is indicated in a rectangular box.

| INCREASE B BY 85. | LET C = B + 38 | PRINT OUT THE VALUES OF P, Q, AND R. |

A diamond box is used for decision making. In it a yes-no question is asked.

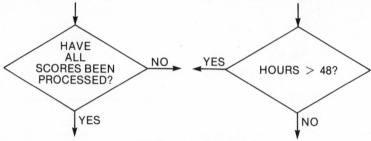

The plan given in a flowchart may be quite complicated, so that following it may be a considerable chore. A calculator is often a useful aid. Also helpful is constructing a table. Study the flow-chart given to the right and the table below. Notice that the table contains one column for each variable in the flowchart.

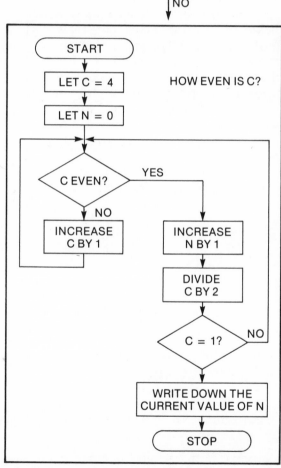

C	N	REMARKS
4		LET C = 4
4	0	LET N = 0
4	1	IF C EVEN, INCREASE N BY 1
2	1	DIVIDE C BY 2
2	2	C ≠ 1 SO N IS INCREASED BY 1
1	2	DIVIDE C BY 2

Exercise Set 5.5

1. Trace through the above flowchart after the second box is changed to:

   a. LET C = 3   b. LET C = 16   c. LET C = 15

2.

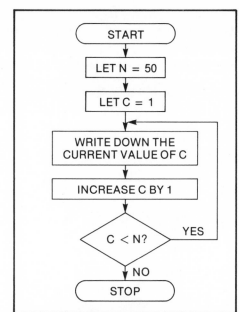

START

LET N = 50

LET C = 1

WRITE DOWN THE
CURRENT VALUE OF C

INCREASE C BY 1

C < N?   YES

NO

STOP

Follow the flowchart given to the left. Explain in simple English what problem it solves. What problem would be solved if the box "Increase C by 1" were changed to "Increase C by 2"?

3. Follow the flowchart. Explain in English what problem is being solved. Change the second box to B = 7, and follow the flowchart again.

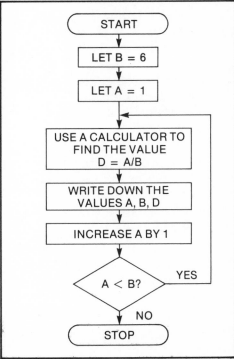

START

LET B = 6

LET A = 1

USE A CALCULATOR TO
FIND THE VALUE
D = A/B

WRITE DOWN THE
VALUES A, B, D

INCREASE A BY 1

A < B?   YES

NO

STOP

4. Carry out the directions of this flowchart for each of these values.
   a. V = 35   b. V = − 23   c. V = − 948   d. V = 316
   What problem does this flowchart solve?

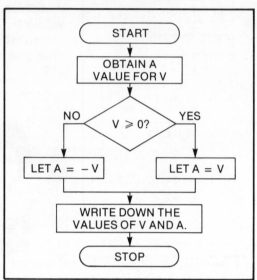

5. a. Make tables for the cases A = 7, B = 2, and A = 12, B = 4.

   b. What problem is solved by the procedure in the flowchart to the right?

   c. Follow the flowchart (with or without a table) for the case A = 5, B = 0, and explain the results.

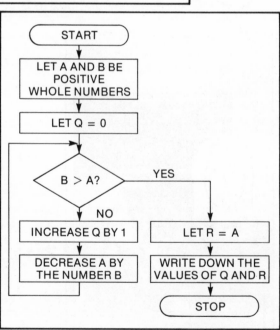

6. A palindromic number is one that reads the same from left to right and right to left. Examples include 31,413 and 728,827. The following five-step plan will always produce a palindromic number. Try it for two different starting values. Then draw a flowchart to represent this plan.
   1. Pick any 2-digit number.
   2. Reverse the digits.
   3. Add the two numbers.
   4. Is it palindromic? If yes, stop.
   5. If not, go back to step 2 with the number you now have.

7. The number 6,174 is a four-digit Jordanian number. It is the "answer" produced by the following procedure.

   1. Select any four-digit number with at least two different digits.

   2. Arrange the digits from largest to smallest to make a number, and from smallest to largest to make a number.

   3. Subtract the smaller number from the larger.

   4. If the answer is 6,174, stop. Otherwise, use the answer as the starting number in step 2.

   | Example: |
Begin with 7083.
8730
− 0378
8352
8532
− 2358
6174
7641
− 1467
6174

   Test the procedure for several different four-digit numbers. Then draw a flowchart for this procedure.

8. Calculate $\sqrt{17}$ to three decimal place accuracy by using a guess and check procedure on the equation $n^2 - 17 = 0$. Then draw a flowchart for the procedure you used.

9. Draw a flowchart for a guess and check procedure for calculating the cube root of a given number, to one decimal place accuracy. Use your flowchart to find $\sqrt[3]{29}$ to one decimal place accuracy.

SIX
Calculator Applications in the Classroom: Motivation & Basic Facts

So far, in the first five chapters, you have focused on the characteristics of the four-function calculator — what these features are and how to use them. You have studied formulas, functions, and problem-solving procedures and how they relate to the calculator. In addition, you have applied your knowledge to classroom settings and evaluated your own understanding of the material by solving problems and writing papers.

In this and the following chapter you will have the opportunity to expand your knowledge of calculator applications in the classroom. You will learn how the calculator may be used as a motivational tool to capture the interest of students and encourage them to learn mathematics and other subjects. Also, you will study alternate ways the calculator may be used to develop and evaluate knowledge of "basic facts." Here, we use the term "basic facts" to mean the set of procedures students learn which help them become skillful in fundamental arithmetic computations. In Chapter 7 you will continue your exploration of classroom applications by studying suggestions and activities in the areas of number theory and problem solving.

The suitability of particular applications depends on your educational goals and the grade level of students you teach or want to teach. No attempt has been made to group the material by grade level. You will find that many applications are suitable over a wide range of levels.

As you progress through these chapters, keep in mind the interactive process of the calculator with mathematics learning. You will have the opportunity through exercises and classroom activities to examine and assess the calculator's role in the curriculum. Whether the curriculum should be restructured substantially to accommodate the calculator or whether the study of mathematics should essentially remain unchanged are issues you will be asked to respond to in detail.

6.1 Making the Calculator "Speak"

People of all ages enjoy using a calculator to form words. When the screen display of a calculator is viewed upside down, most of the numbers look like letters.

CALCULATOR DIGIT	0	1	2	3	4	5	6	7	8	9
UPSIDE-DOWN DIGIT	0	1	z	E	h	5	9	L	B	–

Thus, the upside-down calculator alphabet consists of the nine letters o, i, z, e, h, s, g, l, and b. These letters can be formed into words such as "holes," "shell," and "oil."

Find the answers to the following questions by performing the required calculations. Read the answer upside down on your calculator.

- What did the cannibal cook say when asked where the lost explorer was?

    To find out: Find the product of 6 and 4,759.
                        Add .17 and then double your answer.

- What did the Red Baron put in Snoopy's house?

    To find out: Multiply one hundred and one by the square of three. Add fifty. Multiply the result by each of the whole numbers between six and nine exclusively.

- What did Amelia Earhart's father say the first time he saw her flying an airplane by herself?

    To find out: Find .023 × 3. Add 10,141 to the result. Multiply by 5.

- What does Billie Jean King do to win her tennis matches?

    To find out: Find the square of 11. Subtract 15.521. Multiply by 5. Multiply by the square root of 121.

Many mathematicians and computer scientists feel that the use of calculators to form words is not educationally sound. But, using a calculator in this way has considerable educational merit. For example:

It is fun. Students gain experience in working with calculators and enjoy doing it.

Students learn that electronic machines can work with letters as well as numbers. Since this is fundamental to computer usage, it is a worthwhile achievement.

Students read and follow written directions, using a machine as an aid. Student and machine work together to solve a word problem.

Students can create their own problems and are encouraged to do so. Many students are strongly motivated to be creative by this type of exercise.

To summarize, the calculator letter exercises have many educational values. They illustrate both teaching about calculators and teaching using calculators. Some sample calculator word activities are given below.

Classroom Application Set 6.1

These activities are designed to be used individually with elementary and middle school students or as part of a lesson in which the calculator is made to "speak."

1. Make a list of all two letter calculator words (go, be, oh, ...). Make use of a dictionary as needed.

2. Have the whole class work together to produce a large list of calculator words. This project may extend over a period of weeks. The list can be posted. After the initial list has been created give a student special recognition for finding a new word.

3. The word "geologizes" is 10 letters long and consists entirely of calculator letters. It could be displayed on a ten-digit calculator. Find additional words or phrases that use 10 or more calculator letters.

4. Given a clue and a calculation, find the corresponding word answer.

CLUE	CALCULATION	WORD ANSWER
a. Old Mother _____ when she wanted to wander . . .	$(123^2 \times 2) + 4{,}748$	_____
b. Capitol of state famous for "famous potatoes"	$(789 \times 32) + (340 \times 29)$	_____
c. Big pigs	$4 \times (34^2 + 245)$	_____
d. Slept like a _____	$(987 - 683.5) \times 2$	_____
e. Letters with windows in envelopes	$52{,}818 + 70^2$	_____
f. Snail's home	$281^2 - (101 \times 16)$	_____
g. Get down on your knees and _____	$(54{,}321 \div 3) - (647 \times 27)$	_____
h. They are found in belfries	$(29 \times 146) + 1{,}210^2 - 1{,}410{,}596$	_____
i. Santa Claus drives one	$434{,}343 + (2 \times 13{,}516)$	_____
j. You wouldn't be so sweet, honey, if it weren't for ____	$(10 \times 529) + (1{,}728 \div 36)$	_____

5. Calculator-word "story problems" are created by working backwards from the desired answer. The word "holes" corresponds to the calculator number 53,704. One can get 53,704 in many ways.

$$33{,}333 + 20{,}371 = 53{,}704$$
$$4 \times 13{,}426 = 53{,}704$$
$$161{,}112 \div 3 = 53{,}704$$

Select one of these, such as $33{,}333 + 20{,}371 = 53{,}704$. The 33,333 can be described as "a number consisting of a sequence of five 3's." What can we do with 20,371 to make it more interesting? It could be described as follows. Take the number of pounds in a ton, multiply it by 10, and add 371. The number 371 is $19^2 + 10$. Putting all of this together, we make up a story.

Terry has a new pet, a mole. Terry's father is quite upset. To see why: Add 10 to the square of the century number Abraham

Lincoln lived in. Add 10 times the number of pounds in a ton. Add the number consisting of a sequence of five 3's.

Select a calculator word and make up a story problem for it. Try it out on a classmate.

6. Make up two different calculator story problems that each produce the phrase "he.lies." (Note: the period between *he* and *lies* is actually the decimal point in the answer to the calculation.)

Exercise Set 6.1

These exercises, as well as the exercises in the remaining exercise sets of this chapter, are to be done as part of your study of calculator applications in the classroom.

1. Do Application 1 in the previous set. Compare your list with the one prepared by a colleague.

2. Do Applications 4 and 5 in the previous set. Try to make your problem for Application 5 as interesting as possible by using a variety of calculator operations and applying facts from other subject areas.

3. Make a list of skills one uses when making up calculator-word "story problems." Summarize your list and use this summary to make one or more general statements which support the use of this activity with students.

4. Several companies now make calculators with both numeric and alphabetic keys. The screen can display both letters and numbers when viewed right side up. The calculator memory can store a number of words (or numbers) and retains them after the calculator is switched off. Discuss the advantages and disadvantages of this "scratch pad" memory calculator (which may cost $60 and store up to 30 eight-character words) versus a small note pad and pencil.

6.2 Playing Games with Calculators

The past few years have seen the publication of a considerable number of books of calculator games and puzzles. While many have been written by educators, their primary goal is to entertain. However, every calculator game has educational value — even if it is merely practice in working with numbers and a calculator. Some calculator games have considerable educational merit and are well worth including in the curriculum.

We have already presented one example of calculator games, the formation of words using the upside-down display. A teacher runs some risk that this game may get out of hand. You will know this is beginning to happen when a student calculates $(25 \times 323) + .14$ and leaves the calculator where you will be sure to see it.

In many calculator games the real educational payoff comes after the same game is played a number of times. Students develop strategies for playing the game, and from this process comes generalizations about numbers.

Thus, a reasonable plan to follow is to introduce games and allow students to play them briefly, but frequently, over a two- to three-week period. Generate interest through posted variations of games students develop, problems about games, and tournaments in which the whole class, or portions of it, are involved. In addition, introduce games at appropriate intervals to emphasize various aspects of the curriculum. This strategy allows calculator games to be real teaching aids, capable of motivating students and unlocking their native curiosity and enthusiasm.

Classroom Application Set 6.2

These calculator games are best introduced by playing them with the entire class, or by playing them with a student in front of the entire class. This gives students a "feel" for the games they cannot get by just reading the instructions at an interest center. After the demonstrations have been performed and the rules have been explained, allow students to begin immediately by playing the games in pairs or in small groups.

1. **Nim.** Two players work together on one calculator. A target number such as 21 is selected. The calculator is cleared. Students take turns adding in 1, 2, or 3. The first person to reach or exceed the target number *loses.* Some variations:

   a. First person to reach or exceed the target wins.

   b. Use a larger target number and select the number to be added from the list 1, 4, 7.

   c. Start at a positive number and work backward by subtraction. The target is zero.

2. **Down to zero.** Select a number several digits in length and key it in. For example, 749. A "turn" consists of pushing the $\boxed{-}$ key, pushing a single digit key as many times as desired, and pushing the $\boxed{=}$ key. The goal is to reach zero in as few turns as possible. If a negative answer is reached, you lose.

		DISPLAY
Begin		749
Turn 1:	$\boxed{-}$ $\boxed{6}$ $\boxed{6}$ $\boxed{6}$ $\boxed{=}$	83
Turn 2:	$\boxed{-}$ $\boxed{4}$ $\boxed{4}$ $\boxed{=}$	39
Turn 3:	$\boxed{-}$ $\boxed{3}$ $\boxed{3}$ $\boxed{=}$	6
Turn 4:	$\boxed{-}$ $\boxed{6}$ $\boxed{=}$	0

With the above rules it is evident that an n-digit game can be completed in n or less turns. Some variations on this game follow.

   a. Two players take turns. First person to reach zero wins.

   b. The digit selected in a turn must be one of the digits currently in the calculator display.

3. **Reverse.** A student keys in a two-digit positive integer, with the two digits different. A second student mentally calculates what to add or subtract to produce, as an answer, the original number with its digits reversed. For example, 37 is "reversed" to 73 by adding 36, while 54 is "reversed" to 45 by subtracting 9. The second student uses the calculator to check his or her assertion. Players alternate in making up beginning numbers. Variations:

   a. Use as a target the number 55 rather than the reversed number.

   b. Work with three-digit numbers.

   c. Work with four-digit numbers.

4. **Single digit key.** All of the digit keys on your calculator are broken except the $\boxed{4}$ key. Can you make the display show the number 17? What is the smallest number of keystrokes needed?

Variations:

a. Any target number (not just 17) may be selected.

b. A single digit other than 4 may be used as the digit key that functions.

c. If a calculator has a four-key memory, its use may be allowed.

d. Allow two different digit keys to be functional.

e. Have one of the operation keys, such as $\boxed{+}$, also be broken.

5. **Mental square root.** Name a three-digit number such as 492. Your opponent tries to mentally select an integer n such that n^2 is less than or equal to your number, but $(n + 1)^2$ exceeds your number. If your opponent guesses 22 then one can check that 22^2 = 484 is less than 492, and $(22 + 1)^2 = 23^2 = 529$ exceeds 492. In this case your opponent scores a point. If your opponent guesses lower or higher than 22, you score a point. Take turns specifying the initial number. Variations:

a. Work with two-digit initial numbers for younger students.

b. Require the guess n to be such that $(n - 2)^2$ is less than the given number while $(n + 2)^2$ exceeds it.

c. Play the original game, or a variation of it, for cube roots or fourth roots.

6. **Mental addition and subtraction.** This game is played by two or more students with one calculator. The first student keys in a two-digit number and says a (different) two-digit number out loud. By a single addition or subtraction, the next person is to change the calculator display to this number. The second person then names a (different) two-digit number and passes the calculator on. A single error eliminates a person. As skill develops one can have time limits, such as 10 seconds per turn. Example, with three players:

First player keys in $\boxed{8}$ $\boxed{2}$ and says 45.

Second player keys in $\boxed{-}$ $\boxed{3}$ $\boxed{7}$ $\boxed{=}$, so 45 is displayed, and says 99.

Third player keys in $\boxed{+}$ $\boxed{5}$ $\boxed{4}$ $\boxed{=}$, so 99 is displayed and says 18.

First player keys in $\boxed{-}$ $\boxed{7}$ $\boxed{1}$ $\boxed{=}$, so 28 is displayed. The first player is eliminated, and the game continues.

a. For younger children, play the game with one-digit numbers.

b. For students who are quite good at mental arithmetic, play the game with three-digit numbers.

7. **Taking Aim.** A single student or a group of students may play this game with one calculator. To begin the game, select a target number and a multiplication constant. Key the constant into the machine. (Do not press C at any time during the game, since clearing the machine will force the constant to disappear.) The object is to make the target number, or the target and a decimal, appear on the display screen. For example, let the target be 1,000 and the constant be 27. Key in ☐2 ☐7 ☒ ☐= . Then make a guess, say 30. Thus, key in ☐3 ☐0 ☐= . This gives 810 — too small. Next, try 40. This gives 1,080 — too large. After several more tries, 37.05 is found to work, since 1,000.35 appears on the screen. (Notice that many other numbers will also work. In fact, all numbers n, such that 37.04 ≤ n ≤ 37.07, will produce the target number and a decimal.) The student who first makes the target number appear on the display screen wins the game.
   Variations:
   a. For younger students, limit target numbers to exact multiples of constants. For example, for the target number 72, constants could be 6, 8, or 12.
   b. For students with a good understanding of decimals, select small target numbers and large constants.

8. **Looking For One.** This game is played by two students with one calculator. To begin the game, students agree upon numerical limits, say 1 and 100. One student, without the knowledge of the other selects a number within these limits, say 38, and keys it into the calculator followed by ☐÷ ☐= , thus creating a division constant. (Be careful not to press C at any time during a turn. Clearing the machine will wipe out this constant.) The second student attempts to discover the "mystery number" by keying numbers followed by ☐= . The number "1" will appear on the display screen when the "mystery number" is discovered. Suppose the second student keys in ☐5 ☐0 ☐= on the first try. This gives 1.3157894, indicating 50 is too large. Next, the student tries 35. This gives 0.9210526 — too small. After two more tries 38 gives "1." Each attempt carries the score of one point. Thus, in this example, the second student scores four points. Students keep their own scores. After five turns each, scores are compared. The student with the least number of points wins the game.
   Variations:
   a. For younger students, limit "mystery numbers" to between 1 and 10.

b. For students with good estimation skills, use three- and four-digit "mystery numbers."

9. **Flipnum.** Calculator digits 1, 0, 2, 5, and 8 are the same viewed on the display screen upside down as they are right side up. They are called *flipdigs.* Numbers made up of flipdigs, such as 22, 585, 2,112, and 20,802, are called *flipnums.* They read the same on a calculator upside down as right side up. Two other digits, 6 and 9 are not flipdigs. But, they can be used to make flipnums. The game begins by selecting a target number such as 300. Students two or more) take turns on one calculator displaying flipnums larger than the previously displayed flipnum, but less that the target; begin with the smallest three-digit flipnum. (Two-digit flipnums can be used, but they are relatively routine and uninteresting.) One point is scored for each correct flipnum. Variations:

a. Select up to eight-digit target numbers.
b. Any flipnum skipped and recovered is scored two points.
c. Limits are selected. For example, possible flipnums must be between 10,000 and 11,000.
d. Each successive flipnum must be 100 or more than the previous one.
e. *Addition and Subtraction Flipnum* Limits are selected. The first student keys in a flipnum and passes the calculator to the next student. The second student declares a number that when added (or subtracted) will make a flipnum within the limits. If correct, the second student scores one point. For example, 121 + 30 = 151 and 585 − 80 = 505. If incorrect, the same flipnum is used with the next student. Flipnums are recorded to avoid repeated use. Time limits may be imposed, but should be used with care.

10. **Calculator Jeopardy.** Compared with preceeding games, this game is sophisticated and complex. It may be palyed by two students or two teams of students. Materials need to be constructed. But, you and your students can do this easily. First, select several mathematical categories which are appropriate for your students, such as small whole numbers, large whole numbers, easy decimals, difficult decimals, percentages, short stories, and use-the-memory problems. Then, make ten or more cards for each category. On each card print one number and one or more operations, such as 62 + or 0.75 × + . (Cards containing a single arithmetic operation are worth one point each. Cards with two opera-

tions are worth two points.) One side starts the game by selecting a category and a card from that category. Suppose a student from the first side selected easy decimals for two points and drew the card $\boxed{0.75 \times +}$. To get two points, the student must ask a mathematical question in which two operations are used, $\times$ and $+$, and the answer is 0.75. There are many correct questions. One is: what is $0.8 \times 0.9 + 0.03$? Points are awarded when the opposing student (or student from the opposing team) verifies that the operation(s) on the card is(are) used and the number on the card answers the question. Students may use calculators for generating questions and verifying answers. The student (or team) to receive a previously agreed upon number of points is the winner. Variations:

a. Rank categories in terms of difficulty with questions from more difficult categories assigned larger point values.

b. Place restrictions on the use of calculators. For example, do not allow students to use calculators until questions they ask are completely phrased.

11. **Knick-knack-know.** This game is a calculator variation of the game tic-tac-toe. It is played by two students with one or two calculators on a grid such as the following:

Thirty or more cards, each containing a problem on one side and the answer on the other side, need to be developed. (Students can do this as a math activity.) The game begins as the first student selects a problem card and computes the answer. If the student's answer agrees with the answer on the card, the student is permitted to place an X in the desired box on the grid. If the computed answer is incorrect, an X is not placed and the second student takes a turn using O's. The game is played until one student is able to place X's or O's in three vertical, horizontal, or diagonal boxes. Variations:

a. Select a category for the set of problem cards. For example, construct a set entitled Knick-Knack-Know Decimals or Knick-Knack-Know Metric Measurement.

b. Develop more difficult cards for the center box.

    c. Construct problem-card sets with various difficulties so that students of different ability levels may compete.

    d. Set up a Knick-Knack-Know Tournament.

Exercise Set 6.2

1. Select five of the calculator games presented in this section and play them with a friend or colleague. Do as many of the suggested variations as possible.

2. Choose six of the calculator games from this section. Assess the difficulty of each game and its variations, or otherwise place each game at an appropriate grade level. Compare your results with those of a colleague.

3. For each of the calculator games, determine its best fit in the school mathematics curriculum and explain what each game teaches. How would you use them in your teaching?

4. If you have a group of students available, select two games that are appropriate for their ability level and teach them how to play the games. Then, allow them to play the games. Observe this activity closely and write a brief paper which relates:

    a. Students' reactions to the games.

    b. Suggestions, if any, for altering the games.

5. Using the games presented in this section and others you may know of as a base, write your own calculator game. Be sure:

    a. The object is clearly stated.

    b. The rules are explicit.

    c. The variations, if any, follow from the body of instruction.

6. Reflecting on your answers to the above questions, write a brief statement about the motivational and instructional qualities of calculator games. Should they be considered as a valid part of the mathematics experiences students have in school?

6.3 Opening The Door To The Real World

When students study math in schools, their understanding of and enthusiasm for mathematics is often limited by artificial "real-life" applications they confront in their textbooks. Textbook problems, which propose situations that have little to do with the dynamics of students' daily lives and which always come out *evenly*, seldom promote the idea that mathematics is a useful tool for solving problems important to everyday life.

The calculator, however, allows you and your students to get away from the synthetic numbers and over-simplified situations found in most standard textbooks and become involved in solving real-world problems outside the doors of your classroom. The following application set introduces several ideas for the development of real-world problems which you and your students can construct.

Classroom Application Set 6.3

Each of these applications can be modified for use with an individual student, a small group, or the entire class. All problems require additional information. In some cases you will need to help students identify what information is needed and where it can be found. After this information is located, students will be able to solve the problems with very little additional help. Problems 5 and 6 are more difficult than the rest. They should be used with capable students or as part of a mini-research unit on energy costs.

1. *Why Do You Get Hungry?*
   This activity is designed to provide motivation for the study of health and nutrition. With the calculator, students can compute caloric intake and expenditure easily. Activity:
   a. Determine the number of calories consumed in a recent meal.
      Source: Book on nutrition or diet.
   b. Find the number of calories used in various physical activities such as walking, jogging, riding a bike, doing math, dancing, and sleeping.
      Source: Book on physical education and exercise.

c. Compute the time needed to burn the calories consumed in part (a) when performing the activities, or a combination of the activities, in part (b).

2. *How Much Advertising Do You Watch?*
Television is a major leisure-time activity for many students. This calculator application enables students to find out how much time they watch TV and what percentage of that time is occupied in watching advertisements. Activity:

a. Time the number of minutes you watch TV in an average week.
Source: Students record TV time themselves.

b. Time the number of minutes of commercial advertisements during this period.
Source: Students record commercial time themselves.

c. Estimate the total time you would watch TV in a year, in your lifetime. Calculate the percentage of time you would watch commercials in a week, in a year, in your lifetime. Compute totals and averages for the entire class.

3. *How Much Of This World Is Yours?*
This activity may be used to motivate the study of measurement, area, volume, or perhaps even geography. It is based on the need of students to understand the physical dimensions of their environment. Activity:

a. Determine the area of the floor (floor space) for the part of your home which you call your own.
Source: Students measure using metric or English units or both.

b. Find the floor space for your entire home. Calculate the percentage of your home you call your own.
Source: Students measure using metric or English units or both.

c. Do the same for volume

d. Determine the floor space and volume of your classroom and school. How much of this space is *theoretically* yours?

This activity, and the percentages involved, can be extended to include: house to block, block to city, city to state, state to nation, nation to continent, and finally, continent to world.

4. *What Do These Bikes Cost?*
This is a community-based activity. It is designed to motivate the study of the economic role of the student as a consumer. Activity:

a. Determine the total retail cost of all bikes for sale in the stores of your neighborhoos, community, town or city.
   Source: Direct or telephone contact with store managers.
b. Using recent population figures, estimate the total cost of bikes in your county, in your state.

This activity may be modified easily to enable students to find the total costs of other items such as records, athletic shoes, and comic books.

5. *How Much Does It Cost To Light Up Your Life?*
   This calculator activity is designed to motivate either a science lesson on electricity or a social studies lesson on energy costs or both. Activity:
   a. To operate a stereo for 1 hour, 3½ hours, 8 hours.
      Source: Electrical usage printed on stereo machine. Cost of electrical power available from local utility company.
   b. To run a hair dryer on the highest setting for 10 minutes, 15 minutes, 30 minutes.
      Source: Electrical usage printed on hair dryer, local utility.
   c. To cook a frozen pizza in your oven at 350°F for 30 minutes.
      Source: Usage printed on name plate or in owner's manual of the stove, local utility.
   d. To heat a gallon of water from 40°F to 125°F.
      Source: Local utility company.

6. *What Is The Cost Of Warmth?*
   This application may be used as part of a science lesson on energy: its sources and uses. Also, it may be used to motivate the study of the domestic economy: its dependence on energy. In either case, the calculator is a useful tool for computing the large numbers involved. Activity:

   > Compute the comparative costs of heating a room the size of your classroom with electricity, gas, oil, coal, or wood to 65°F for 3,550 degree days.*

   > Source: Distributors of each product for current unit prices.
   >   U.S. Department of Energy, or its representative, for data on the amount of energy required to heat a room the size of your classroom one degree day.

   *Degree days represents the cumulative total number of degrees by which the average daily temperature falls below 65 degrees Fahrenheit. The number 3,550 was the average number of degree days in the United States for the year 1979-80 according to the Center for Environmental Assessment Services, National Oceanic and Atmospheric Administration.

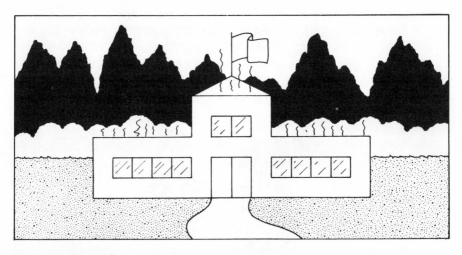

Exercise Set 6.3

1. Perform two of the calculator classroom applications in this section. Consult the suggested sources for information needed to do the problems. From this experience predict how long it would take students at the appropriate ability level to do the same problems.

2. Place each of the six classroom applications in this section at an appropriate grade-level range (i.e., grades 3-5, grades 7-8, etc.). Then explain how you would use each of them in your teaching. Compare your answers with the answers of a colleague. How are they similar? How do they differ? Why?

3. Select an application which you did not do in Ex. 1. Identify an appropriate grade level and a specific lesson for which you would use the problem. Then reconstruct the problem accordingly. Be sure you:

   a. Address student's real-life experiences and interests.

   b. State the activities and source suggestions explicitly.

   c. Show that the application is an integral part of the lesson.

4. If you have a group of students available, perform the application and the lesson you developed in Ex. 3 with them. Then write a brief report which relates:

   a. Students' interest in and enthusiasm for the lesson.

   b. The benefits of including the application in the lesson.

   c. Modifications, if any, to the application and/or lesson.

5. Energy, pollution, and inflation are concerns (real-world problems) of every adult. But, do these problems concern elementary and middle school students? Talk with a group of students and try to assess what is important to them. What do they consider to be real-world problems?

6. Write a brief paper which illustrates the motivational and instructional qualities of real-world problems. Your paper should include:

   a. A definition of the term "real-world problem."

   b. Your perception of how real-world problems should be developed and used. Make specific reference to the use of calculators.

6.4 Learning Basic Operations on the Calculator

The four-function calculator with algebraic logic and a built-in constant function is an effective aid in helping students learn basic addition, subtraction, multiplication, and division facts. Classroom applications which follow suggest ways the calculator may be used in drill of operations and decimal equivalents, analysis of algorithms, and exploration of negative numbers and powers.

Classroom Application Set 6.4

1. *Basic Operations Drill*

    In this application we are assuming your calculator has a built-in constant feature for each of the operations you wish to study. To convert your calculator into an automatic flash card machine, key in a built-in constant. For example, keying in $\boxed{5}$ $\boxed{+}$ $\boxed{=}$ puts 5 and + in the calculator's memory. This adds 5 to any number keyed in and followed by $\boxed{=}$. Thus, when $\boxed{5}$ $\boxed{+}$ $\boxed{=}$ is keyed, $\boxed{9}$ $\boxed{=}$ produces 14, $\boxed{6}$ $\boxed{=}$ gives 11, and $\boxed{2}$ $\boxed{1}$ $\boxed{=}$ makes 26. Subtraction, multiplication, and division work exactly the same way. Keying in $\boxed{4}$ $\boxed{-}$ $\boxed{=}$ subtracts the constant 4, $\boxed{7}$ $\boxed{\times}$ $\boxed{=}$ multiplies by the constant 7, and $\boxed{2}$ $\boxed{\div}$ $\boxed{=}$ divides the number, keyed in and followed by $\boxed{=}$, by the constant 2. Activity:

    a. Develop a simple check sheet (similar to the one below) which students can use to record the correctness of answers for basic operations drill.

	5 +	4 −	7 ×	2 ÷
1				
2				
3				
4				
5				

This sample check sheet provides for five numbers and four different constants and operations.

    b. Use the check sheet you developed in part (a) with students individually. Students begin by first keying in constants such as $\boxed{5}$ $\boxed{+}$ $\boxed{=}$. Next, they key in the first number in the column on the left. Then, they say the answer out loud and check by pressing $\boxed{=}$. If correct, students place a check in the corresponding box.

This activity may be varied by keying in the constants and requiring students to discover which constants were keyed in. Students enjoy doing this in pairs.

2. *Decimal Equivalents Drill*
   The built-in constant function for ÷ transforms your calculator into an automatic flash card machine which produces the decimal equivalents of common fractions. For example, to find the decimal equivalents for the fractions ⅛, ⅜, ⅜, . . ., ⅞, key in 8 ÷ = . Then, press 1 = , 2 = , 3 = , . . ., 7 = . Activity:
   a. Using your calculator, complete the following table of decimal equivalents. The numbers along the top of the table represent numerators. Numbers in the column on the left represent denominators.

D \ N	1	2	3	4	5
6					
5					
4					
3					
2					

   b. To perform drill in decimal equivalents, use the table above as a check sheet. Follow the procedure outlined in Application 1(b) in this set.

3. *Analysis of Algorithms*
   Rather than serving to eliminate the need for learning basic algorithms, the calculator can be a useful tool to help students understand these algorithms. This activity not only leads students to take a closer look at why algorithms work as they do, but it also suggests alternate ways for performing arithmetical operations. Activity:
   a. Find the missing numbers. Use your calculator.

```
   687          600         80          7
 + 245        + 200       + 40        + 5
 _____       _____     _____     _____
[      ]     [      ] + [      ] + [      ] = [      ]

   546          500         30         16
 - 129        - 100       - 20        - 9
 _____       _____     _____     _____
[      ]     [      ] + [      ] + [      ] = [      ]
```

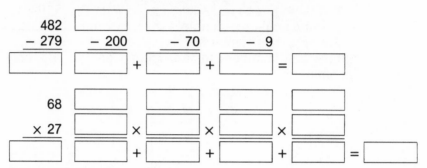

| 36 | 6 | 30 | 6 | 30 |
| × 18 | × 8 | × 8 | × 10 | × 10 |

☐   ☐ + ☐ + ☐ + ☐ = ☐

b. Make these work. Check using your calculator.

482   ☐ ☐ ☐
− 279   − 200   − 70   − 9

☐   ☐ + ☐ + ☐ = ☐

68   ☐ ☐ ☐ ☐
× 27   ☐ × ☐ × ☐

☐   ☐ + ☐ + ☐ + ☐ = ☐

4. *Exploring Negative Numbers*

Many inexpensive calculators have a change-sign key, labeled ⎡+/−⎤. To key in a negative number, such as − 6, simply press ⎡6⎤ ⎡+/−⎤. Negative numbers, such as − 6 and − 8, may be added by pressing ⎡6⎤ ⎡+/−⎤ ⎡+⎤ ⎡8⎤ ⎡+/−⎤ ⎡=⎤. In fact, all operations work exactly the same for negative numbers as for positive numbers. But, you must remember to press ⎡+/−⎤ after each number you wish to make negative. (Note: to generate negative numbers on some calculators, ⎡+/−⎤ may be pressed before the number.) Activity:

a. Perform the following on your calculator.

a. − 6 + − 6 = ☐   f. − 31 + 16 = ☐

b. − 4 + − 9 = ☐   g. − 14 + 41 = ☐

c. − 8.6 + − 10 = ☐   h. 16 + − 15 = ☐

d. − 12 + 2 = ☐   i. 62 + − 21 = ☐

e. 18 + − 6 = ☐

What do you think is always true about the sum of two negative numbers? What can you say about the sum of a negative number and a positive number?

b. Calculate the following in order.

a. $^-3 - 2 =$ ⬚

f. $^-3 - ^-3 =$ ⬚

b. $^-3 - 1 =$ ⬚

g. $^-3 - ^-4 =$ ⬚

c. $^-3 - 0 =$ ⬚

h. $^-3 - ^-5 =$ ⬚

d. $^-3 - ^-1 =$ ⬚

i. $^-3 - ^-6 =$ ⬚

e. $^-3 - ^-2 =$ ⬚

Do you see a pattern develop? What sort of general statement can you make from your observation?

c. Do the following in order on your calculator. Key in $\boxed{2}$ $\boxed{+/-}$ $\boxed{\times}$ $\boxed{=}$ as constants.

a. $^-2 \times 4 =$ ⬚

f. $^-2 \times ^-1 =$ ⬚

b. $^-2 \times 3 =$ ⬚

g. $^-2 \times ^-2 =$ ⬚

c. $^-2 \times 2 =$ ⬚

h. $^-2 \times ^-3 =$ ⬚

d. $^-2 \times 1 =$ ⬚

i. $^-2 \times ^-4 =$ ⬚

e. $^-2 \times 0 =$ ⬚

What is the pattern that develops? Make a general statement about the product of negative numbers.

5. *Exploring Powers*
The built-in constant function allows positive and negative numbers to be raised to nonnegative whole-number powers. For example, 12^2 is computed on the calculator by pressing $\boxed{1}$ $\boxed{2}$ $\boxed{\times}$ $\boxed{=}$, $^-6^3$ is keyed in as $\boxed{6}$ $\boxed{+/-}$ $\boxed{\times}$ $\boxed{=}$ $\boxed{=}$, and $^-1.9^5$ is calculated by pressing $\boxed{1}$ $\boxed{.}$ $\boxed{9}$ $\boxed{+/-}$ $\boxed{\times}$ $\boxed{=}$ $\boxed{=}$ $\boxed{=}$ $\boxed{=}$. The result is $^-24.76099$. Activity:
a. Calculate the following.

i. $3^3 = \boxed{}$ iv. $2.33^5 = \boxed{}$

ii. $^-4^4 = \boxed{}$ v. $12.4^2 = \boxed{}$

iii. $1.9^6 = \boxed{}$ vi. $^-6.9112^4 = \boxed{}$

b. Find x in each of the following. Use your calculator.

    i. $4^x = 4{,}096$ iv. $1.001^x = 1.011055$
    ii. $22^x = 234{,}256$ v. $246^x = 60{,}516$
    iii. $^-9.37^x = 87.7969$ vi. $^-.5^x = 0.015625$

c. For what values of x is each of the following a true statement, when figured on your calculator.

i. $.01^x = 0$ ii. $^-.22^x = 0$ iii. $.5^x = 0$

d. Using trial-and-error proceedures, find the value of y in each of the following. (In each case y is a whole number.)

i. $y^5 = 3{,}125$ ii. $y^3 = 1$ iii. $y^{10} = 1{,}024$

Exercise Set 6.4

1. Perform each one of the applications in this section. Place each at an appropriate grade-level range (i.e., grades 3-5, grades 7-8, etc.). Then, explain how you could use them in your teaching.

2. The applications in this section outline several of the many ways calculators may be used to strengthen basic facts. Prepare a list of the arguments *in favor* of using calculators to learn basic arithmetic facts. Also, make a list of arguments *against* the use of calculators to learn basic facts. Compare these lists with those of a colleague.

3. In view of the lists you prepared in Ex. 2, write a position paper (appropriate for presentation to a school district curriculum committee) on the role of the calculator as a tool for teaching basic arithmetical facts.

6.5 Mental Approximations and Calculations

Mental approximation, or estimation, is a very important aspect of computation and of problem solving. Skill in mental approximation can be increased by learning and practicing some fundamentals.

Mental approximations depend heavily upon understanding our (base 10) place-value number system. What is 312 + 897?

Think: 312 is approximately the same as 300
             897 is approximately the same as 900

Think: 3 (hundred) + 9 (hundred) = 12 (hundred)

Conclude that the answer is approximately 1,200.

The easiest approach to approximating a number by a multiple of a power of 10 is to change all of the digits after the first to zeros. Examples of *first-digit approximations* are the following:

$$329 \longrightarrow 300$$
$$6{,}894 \longrightarrow 6{,}000$$
$$49 \longrightarrow 40$$
$$150 \longrightarrow 100$$

A more sophisticated approach, which produces more accurate approximations on the average, is *rounding.* Rounding to the first digit produces:

$$329 \longrightarrow 300$$
$$6{,}894 \longrightarrow 7{,}000$$
$$49 \longrightarrow 50$$
$$150 \longrightarrow 200$$

Both first-digit approximation and rounding approximation can be done mentally. With practice they can be done very rapidly.

Mental approximations are useful in all stages of problem solving. Very young students can learn first-digit approximation techniques. Older students can be taught rounding.

Classroom Application Set 6.5

Each of the following applications is designed to be done mentally. Each can also be done on a calculator (or, with paper and pencil). It is instructive to calculate ratios of approximate to exact answers (that is, approximate answer divided by exact answer) to help develop a "feel" for how accurate your approximations are. This is a useful idea in addition, multiplication, and division problems. It may not be useful in some subtraction problems, especially those with exact answers of zero or near zero.

1. Use both first-digit and rounding approximation methods to write approximate answers to the following addition problems.

   a.　78　　　　b.　89　　　　c.　692
   　　+35　　　　　+94　　　　　+841

   　　　　　　　　e.　821
   　　　　　　　　　347
   d.　3,894　　　　　31
   　　+7,265　　　+814

2. Another method of approximation involves *rounding to the most significant digit.* In the following addition problem, the most significant digit is the hundreds digit.

   $$847 \longrightarrow 8 \text{ (hundreds)}$$
   $$29 \longrightarrow 0 \text{ (hundreds)}$$
   $$317 \longrightarrow 3 \text{ (hundreds)}$$
   $$+\ \ 7 \longrightarrow 0 \text{ (hundreds)}$$

   Approximate sum = 11 (hundreds) = 1,100

Give approximate answers to the following by rounding to the most significant digit.

a.   394
     + 49

d.   72
            879
          3,904
            671
        +   9

b.   97
       + 849

c.   8,204
          694
        3,715
           69
      +   187

3. The same general techniques that are used in addition are also useful to approximate answers to subtraction problems. Use first-digit approximation, first-digit rounding, and rounding to the most significant digit to find approximate answers to each of the following:

a.   897   b.   6,987   c. $189 - 147 + 928 - 475$
      − 349   − 3,798   d. $98 + 75 - 87 - 4$
                                     e. $2,047 + 3,174 - 5,029 + 47$

4. Mental approximation in multiplication requires the approximation of each quantity to its most significant digit.

        849   800
      × 63   Is approximated by   ×   60
                                       48,000

Find approximate answers to the following by using the method of rounding to the most significant digit for multiplication.

a.   325   c. $89 \times 47 \times 103$
         × 73   d. $9 \times 62 \times 21$
b.   8,417   e. $841 \times 53 \times 3,018$
        × 675

5. Division approximation is done using the same ideas as in multiplication approximation. But, one often ends up working with fractions. This is a good argument for the need to keep fractions in our curriculum.

$$\frac{847 \longrightarrow 800}{23 \longrightarrow 20} = 40 \qquad \frac{847 \longrightarrow 800}{33 \longrightarrow 30} = \left(\frac{8}{3}\right) \times 10$$

Mentally, one can approximate 8/3 by its nearest whole number 3 and get 30 as an approximate answer in this problem. Use mental arithmetic to find approximate answers to the following.

a. $\dfrac{647}{23}$

b. $9\overline{)9375}$

c. $37\overline{)8249}$

d. $\dfrac{794 + 387}{63}$

e. $\dfrac{8,947 + 6,937}{384 - 147}$

6. An important application of mental approximation is in detecting "obvious" errors made while using a calculator. Find the "obviously" incorrect answers. Check by using your calculator.

a.
$$\begin{array}{r} 817 \\ \times\ \ 31 \\ \hline 254,087 \end{array}$$

f.
$$\begin{array}{r} 125 \\ \times\ 6.7 \\ \hline 837.5 \end{array}$$

k. $\dfrac{621}{89} = .7547806$

b.
$$\begin{array}{r} 98 \\ \times\ 97 \\ \hline 9,506 \end{array}$$

g.
$$\begin{array}{r} 3.922 \\ \times\ 875 \\ \hline 343.175 \end{array}$$

l. $\dfrac{67}{325} = .2061538$

c.
$$\begin{array}{r} 92615 \\ \times\ 41 \\ \hline 3,797,215 \end{array}$$

h.
$$\begin{array}{r} .37 \\ \times\ 9.5 \\ \hline .3515 \end{array}$$

m. $\dfrac{929}{9,874} = .9344744$

n. $\dfrac{36.5}{9.82} = 3.7169042$

d.
$$\begin{array}{r} 98.2 \\ \times\ 3.84 \\ \hline 3,770.88 \end{array}$$

i. $\dfrac{37}{16} = 23.125$

e.
$$\begin{array}{r} 63.8 \\ \times\ 985 \\ \hline 62,843 \end{array}$$

j. $\dfrac{8,295}{45} = 184.33333$

7. It is important that students realize that mental arithmetic is quicker, more convenient, and as accurate as calculator arithmetic for a wide variety of problems. At each grade level students should acquire some additional mental arithmetic skills. Activity:

    Speed and accuracy drill. Select a mental drill sheet which students have mastered. Divide the class in half. One half of the class does the sheet using mental arithmetic. The other half *must* use a calculator. The calculator-using students must key in each problem and copy down the calculator answer. Call off the time in five-second increments so students can record their times. After all students complete the activity, run it a second time with another form of the drill sheet. The mental arithmetic people and calculator users switch roles. Tabulate the results and discuss them with the class.

8. There are many mental arithmetic "tricks" that can be used to increase mental arithmetic skills. These tricks can be discovered and/or practiced on your calculator.

    a. To square a positive whole number ending in 5 take the number to the left of the 5 and multiply it by the next higher integer. The answer to the squaring problem is the answer to this multiplication problem followed by the digits 25.

    $35^2 = ?$ Think: $3 \times 4 = 12$
                    Write down 1,225.
    $205^2 = ?$ Think: $20 \times 21 = 420$
                    Write down 42,025

    b. To multiply a number by 11, multiply it by 10 (that is, add a zero) and then add the original number.

    $15 \times 11 = ?$ Think: 150
                                     +   15
                        Write down   165

    $28 \times 11 = ?$ Think: 280
                                     +   28
                        Write down   308

    c. To see if an integer is evenly divisible by 2, check to see if its unit digit is divisible by 2.

To see if an integer is evenly divisible by 4, check to see if the number in its tens and units place is divisible by 4.

67,942 is not evenly divisible by 4

18,964 is evenly divisible by 4

To see if an integer is evenly divisible by 8, check to see if the number in its hundreds, tens, and units position is divisible by 8.

927,848 is evenly divisible by 8

793,822 is not evenly divisible by 8

To see if an integer is evenly divisible by 3, check to see if the sum of its digits is divisible by 3.

69,315 is evenly divisible by 3

82,412 is not evenly divisible by 3

To see if an integer is evenly divisible by 9, check to see if the sum of its digits is divisible by 9.

819,639 is evenly divisible by 9

981,363 is not evenly divisible by 9

An integer is evenly divisible by 6 if it is even and evenly divisible by 3.

d. Think of numbers near a power of 10 as being that power of 10 plus or minus a correction factor. For example:

$$14 \times 102 = (14 \times 100) + (14 \times 2) = 1,428$$
$$23 \times 97 = (23 \times 100) - (23 \times 3) = 2,231$$
$$96 + 105 + 98 + 107 =$$

$$
\begin{array}{r}
100 - 4 \\
100 + 5 \\
100 - 2 \\
+\ 100 + 7 \\
\hline
400 + 6 = 406
\end{array}
$$

e. The product of a pair of integers differing by 2 is the square of the whole number between them, minus 1. For example:

$$5 \times 7 = 6^2 - 1 = 35$$
$$14 \times 16 = 15^2 - 1 = 224$$
$$19 \times 21 = 20^2 - 1 = 399$$

Exercise Set 6.5

1. Perform applications 1 through 5 in this section. Calculate ratios of approximate to exact answers for several problems from each application. Use these ratios to rank the three methods of

approximation (first-digit approximation, first-digit rounding, and rounding to the most significant digit) from the least to the most accurate.

2. Make a list of the uses of approximation in school mathematics. Include ways in which approximation may be used in solving problems with a calculator.

3. Perform applications 6 through 8 in this section. Develop a work sheet, or a series of work sheets, which give practice in mental arithmetic "tricks." If you have a group of students, give them this material and ask that they check answers with their calculators.

6.6 Decimal Equivalents

Every fraction has a decimal representation which either terminates or repeats. Thus, ½ = .5 (terminates), while ⅓ = .333 ... (repeats). When a calculation is done using a calculator, it may well result in a decimal expansion corresponding to a simple fraction. If so, it is often desirable that the student recognize this fact. For example, if sixteen cupcakes are to be divided among twelve children, each child will get 16 ÷ 12 = 1.3333333 cupcakes. It is desirable to recognize that each child should get 1⅓ cupcakes.

I thought $\frac{16}{24} = \frac{2}{3}$. My calculator says it's .6666666

Classroom Application Set 6.6

1. Use your calculator to find decimal representations for the following fractions. Hint: ½ = (1 ÷ 2) = .5.

a. 1/2	k. 3/5
b. 1/3	l. 3/6
c. 1/4	m. 4/5
d. 1/5	n. 4/6
e. 1/6	o. 5/6
f. 2/3	
g. 2/4	
h. 2/5	
i. 2/6	
j. 3/4	

2. Use your answers to application 1 to write decimal representations for the following numbers. Hint: $4\frac{1}{2} = 4 + \frac{1}{2} = 4 + .5 = 4.5$
   a. $1\frac{1}{2}$
   b. $8\frac{1}{2}$
   c. $4\frac{1}{3}$
   d. $13\frac{1}{3}$
   e. $5\frac{1}{6}$
   f. $8\frac{4}{5}$
   g. $14\frac{3}{4}$
   h. $2\frac{1}{5}$
   i. $6\frac{5}{6}$
   j. $4\frac{3}{4}$
   k. $7\frac{1}{4}$
   l. $12\frac{2}{3}$

3. For each of the following, find two different fractions whose
   calculator decimal representations are:
   a. .3333333 (Solution: $\frac{1}{3}$ and $\frac{2}{6}$, among others)
   b. .15
   c. .25
   d. .6666666
   e. .4
   f. .8333333
   g. .75
   h. 18
   i. .1
   j. .1428571
   k. .4285714

4. A terminating decimal expansion is easily written as a fraction.
   Thus, .25 = 25/100. Sometimes the fraction can be written in a
   simpler form, such as $\frac{1}{4}$ in this case. Write a fraction equal to
   each of the following terminating decimal expansions. Give a
   simpler fraction with the same decimal expansion if possible.
   a. .4 (Solutions = $\frac{4}{10}$ = $\frac{2}{5}$)
   b. .2   f. .1
   c. .5   g. .8
   d. .75   h. .35
   e. .6   i. .45

5. On an eight-digit calculator $\frac{1}{9}$ = .1111111, $\frac{2}{9}$ = .2222222, $\frac{3}{9}$ =
   .3333333, etc. We often represent repeating decimals by "bar"

notation. Thus, $.\overline{1}$ means .1111..., $.\overline{2}$ means .2222..., etc. Find fractions with the following decimal representations.

a. $.\overline{2}$ b. $.\overline{5}$ c. $.\overline{1}$ d. $.\overline{8}$ e. $.\overline{7}$ f. $.\overline{3}$

According to the pattern and ideas in this problem, what fraction corresponds to $.\overline{9}$? What is another, simpler, name for this fraction?

6. Drawing upon ideas from Application 5, express the following using fractional notation.

a. $3.\overline{4}$ (Solution: $.\overline{4}$ is $\%$, so answer is 3%)
b. $8.\overline{1}$
c. $2.\overline{7}$
d. $15.\overline{2}$
e. $3.\overline{3}$
f. $66.\overline{6}$
g. $9.\overline{5}$

7. The decimal representation of ⅟₉₉ is .010101..., often written as $.\overline{01}$. Find decimal representations for ⅟₉₉, ⅖₉₉, ⅗₉₉, ⅘₉₉, etc. until you have the pattern firmly in mind. Use this information to find fractions which have the following decimal representations.

a. $.\overline{01}$
b. $.\overline{05}$
c. $.\overline{12}$
d. $.\overline{45}$
e. $.\overline{98}$
f. $.\overline{10}$
g. $.\overline{50}$
h. $.\overline{56}$
i. $.\overline{33}$

Exercise Set 6.6

1. Find answers to each of the applications in this section. In your estimation, at what grade level would it be appropriate to begin a study of decimal equivalents using calculators? Justify your answer.

2. Make a list of the ways the calculator may be used in the teaching of decimal equivalents. Match appropriate grade levels with each item in your list. Compare your list with the list composed by a colleague.

6.7 Multidigit Multiplication

Observe how the one-digit multiplication facts are used, along with positional notation and addition, to do the following multiplication problem.

```
        5 9 3
      ×   4 7
          2 1  ←——— 7 × 3
          6 3  ←——— 7 × 9
        3 5    ←——— 7 × 5
          1 2  ←——— 4 × 3
        3 6    ←——— 4 × 9
      2 0      ←——— 4 × 5
      2 7,8 7 1
```

Next, analyze how we do a larger problem working with two digits as a time. We use a calculator to perform the two-digit multiplications. In essence, we are doing base 100 arithmetic.

```
        87 69
      ×  3 74
         51 06  ←——— 74 × 69
      64 38     ←——— 74 × 87
       2 07     ←———  3 × 69
      2 61      ←———  3 × 87
      3 27 96 06
```

We can use a calculator to check that the product of 8,769 and 374 is indeed 3,279,606.

This same technique can be used to find exact products in situations that will overflow a calculator. With an eight-digit calculator, we can work with four digits at a time. Study the following example which uses base 10,000 arithmetic.

```
        835 9372
         68 9347
         8760 0084  ←——— 9,347 × 9,372
      780 4745      ←——— 9,347 ×   835
       63 7296      ←———   68 × 9,372
      5 6780        ←———   68 ×   835
      5 7625 0801 0084
```

Notice that a calculator can be used to sum the columns of four-digit numbers, but paper and pencil is probably faster.

One can use scientific notation and a calculator to approximate a multidigit product such as above.

$$8,359,372 = 8.359372 \times 10^6$$
$$689,347 = 6.89347 \times 10^5$$

By use of a calculator, we conclude an approximate product is 57.62508 $\times$ 10^{11} or 5,762,508,000,000. This agrees well with our exact product, giving us increased confidence in our exact product.

Classroom Application Set 6.7

1. Use scientific notation to find approximate answers and use base 10,000 arithmetic to find exact answers for the following.
    a. $12,345,678 \times 87,654,321$
    b. $123,456,789 \times 987,654,321$
    c. $919,293,949,596,979,899 \times 84,927,356$
    d. $(987,654,321)^3$
2. Devise a calculator-assisted method for doing exact multidigit long division. Keep in mind that mutliplication is essentially successive addition and that division is essentially successive subtraction.

Exercise Set 6.7

1. Perform the applications in this section. Explain how you would use them in your teaching.
2. Make a list of topics which are reinforced by multidigit multiplication and division using a calculator. What instructional value do multidigit calculations have when calculators are not used? In your estimation, do calculators make a significant contribution to the study of multidigit calculations? If so, in what way?

SEVEN
Calculator Applications in the Classroom: Understanding Numbers and Problem Solving

The four-function hand-held calculator is a powerful instructional tool. As you observed in Chapter 6, it may be used in the classroom to increase student interest in mathematics and provide students with an additional means to learn and exercise basic facts. This chapter suggests further applications of the calculator in school mathematics instruction. By performing the exercises and the classroom applications you will not only learn how calculators can be used to develop understanding of number properties and patterns, but you will also learn ways in which calculators can be used to assist in the development of problem-solving skill. The chapter concludes with a brief discussion of the potential impact of the calculator on the school curriculum.

Let us begin by examining some number patterns that can be discovered and examined with the use of a calculator.

7.1 Exploring Number Patterns On The Calculator

Students are often fascinated by number patterns which emerge when certain computations are performed. Calculators can make finding these patterns easy and enjoyable because they free students from tedious hand computations. Thus, using calculators to find number patterns achieves two purposes. It gives students the idea that there *is* order in our number system and that discovering this order can be fun, and secondly, it provides for the learning of a lot of mathematics along the way.

When you look at the number pattern 2, 4, 6, 8, 10, your mind "instinctively" fills in the next term, 12. But, some patterns are not this easy to detect. Consider the following:

1, 1, 2, 3, 5, 8, 13, 21	(Fibonacci)
1, 4, 9, 16, 25, 36,	(Squares)

Detecting and describing patterns is an important part of mathematics. Generally, a description adequate to continue to extend the pattern can be done in words. For example "You go up by 2 each time." Later in a student's mathematical career the description becomes more formal, perhaps even using algebraic notation.

Classroom Application Set 7.1

These applications may be used individually or with small groups of students to improve their understanding of the real number system. Alternately, students may use them as a means to have fun with numbers. In either case, you will find students enjoy them and learn some mathematics in the process.

1. Observe:

$$2^2 - 1^2 = 3$$
$$3^2 - 2^2 = 5$$
$$4^2 - 3^2 = 7$$
$$5^2 - 4^2 = 9$$

Calculate:

$$6^2 - 5^2 =$$
$$8^2 - 7^2 =$$

.

.

.

$$15^2 - 14^2 =$$

Describe the pattern. Then mentally calculate $21^2 - 20^2$, $51^2 - 50^2$, and $100^2 - 99^2$. Check using a calculator or by other means.

2. Here are some pattern problems.
   a. Calculate 5^1, 5^2, 5^3, 5^4, 5^5, 5^6, 5^7, 5^8, 5^9. Describe the pattern formed by the units digits in these numbers. What will be the units digit in 5^{100}?
   b. Repeat for 2^1, 2^2, etc. and find the units digit in 2^{100}.
   c. Repeat for 7^1, 7^2, etc. and find the units digit in 7^{100}.
   d. Find the 10's digit in 1^{100}, 2^{100}, and 7^{100}.

3. If your calculator has an automatic constant for multiplication, key in [1] [.] [0] [0] [0] [0] [0] [0] [1] [×] [=] [=] [=] [=] etc. Record and describe the pattern that results. What will the display read if [=] is pushed 500 times? Repeat this application with the right most digit in the initial number being a 2, and then being a 5.

4. Compute the answers to the first few problems below mentally or by use of a calculator. Study the pattern that emerges. Find the remaining answers by extending the pattern. Check mentally or by use of a calculator.

$$1{,}089 \times 1 =$$
$$1{,}089 \times 2 =$$
$$1{,}089 \times 3 =$$
$$1{,}089 \times 4 =$$
$$1{,}089 \times 5 =$$
$$1{,}089 \times 6 =$$
$$1{,}089 \times 7 =$$
$$1{,}089 \times 8 =$$
$$1{,}089 \times 9 =$$

5. Calculate the answers to the first few problems below by use of a calculator. Once you detect a pattern, complete the answers to the problems by extending the pattern. Then, check your guesses.

$$1 \times 8 + 1 = 9$$
$$12 \times 8 + 2 =$$
$$123 \times 8 + 3 =$$
$$1{,}234 \times 8 + 4 =$$
$$12{,}345 \times 8 + 5 =$$
$$123{,}456 \times 8 + 6 =$$
$$1{,}234{,}567 \times 8 + 7 =$$
$$12{,}345{,}678 \times 8 + 8 =$$
$$123{,}456{,}789 \times 8 + 9 =$$

6. The sequence 1, 1, 2, 3, 5, 8, 13, ... is usually known as the Fibonacci sequence, named after the Italian mathematician, Fibonacci. Notice that each term after the second is the sum of the previous two terms.

a. Find the next ten terms.

b. The ratios of successive terms form an interesting sequence:

$$\frac{1}{1} = 1 \qquad \frac{2}{1} = 2 \qquad \frac{3}{2} = 1.5 \qquad \frac{5}{3} = 1.\overline{6}$$

Find the next 12 terms of this sequence. If this sequence is continued indefinitely, its terms will get closer and closer to the
number $(1 + \sqrt{5})/2$, which is sometimes called the Golden Ratio.
Compute the difference between the Golden Ratio and the last
term you calculated above.

7. Compute:
$$1^3 =$$
$$1^3 + 2^3 =$$
$$1^3 + 2^3 + 3^3 =$$
$$1^3 + 2^3 + 3^3 + 4^3 =$$
$$1^3 + 2^3 + 3^3 + 4^3 + 5^3 =$$

Predict: $1^3 + 2^3 + 3^3 + \ldots + 10^3 =$

Hint: The numbers on the right are perfect squares.

8. Observe:
$$2 + 5 + 8 + 11 + 14 + 17 + 20 + 23 + 26 + 29 =$$

$$\left.\begin{array}{c} 2 + 29 \\ 5 + 26 \\ 8 + 23 \\ 11 + 20 \\ + 14 + 17 \end{array}\right\} = 5 \times 31 = 155$$

This pairing "trick" works when summing any sequence in which
the terms always change by a constant amount. Find the
following sums using the pairing technique. Check by use of a
calculator.

a. $5 + 7 + 9 + 11 + 13 + 15 + 17 + 19 + 21 + 23 + 25 + 27$

b. $10 + 15 + 20 + 25 + 30 + 35 + 40 + 45 + 50 + 55$

c. The sum of the first 40 terms of the sequence which starts at
1 and has a difference of 2 between successive terms (i.e., 1, 3,
5, . . .).

d. $8 + 13 + 18 + 23 + 28 + 33 + 38 + 43 + 48$

e. $1 + 2 + 3 + 4 + \ldots + 999 + 1000$ (Do not bother to check
this on a calculator!)

9. Mathematicians often use formulas to describe patterns. The
formula $f(n) = (n)(n + 1)/2$ is the sum of the integers $1 + 2 + 3 +$
$\ldots + n$. For example, the formula gives $f(10) = (10)(11)/2 = 55$.
This is $1 + 2 + 3 + 4 + 5 + 6 + 7 + 8 + 9 + 10$. Use the

formula to find f(20), f(100), f(250), and f(1,000). Check your answers by using the pairing technique of Application 8.

10. A formula for the sum of squares of successive integers is given by:

$$f(n) = \frac{(n)(n + 1)(2n + 1)}{6} = 1^2 + 2^2 + 3^2 + \ldots + n^2$$

For example, $f(5) = (5)(6)(11)/6 = 55$, which is $1^2 + 2^2 + 3^2 + 4^2 + 5^2$. Make use of the formula in solving the following problems. Check by use of a calculator.

a. $1^2 + 2^2 + 3^2 + \ldots + 10^2$

b. $8^2 + 9^2 + 10^2 + \ldots + 15^2$ (Hint: $f(15) - f(7)$)

c. $11^2 + 12^2 + 13^2 + \ldots + 20^2$

Exercise Set 7.1

These exercises are intended to help increase your insight into elementary and middle school uses of calculators.

1. Perform each of the applications in Classroom Application Set 7.1.

2. Rank the applications in Set 7.1 from easiest to most difficult. Determine an appropriate grade level, or grade-level range, for each application. Then, make a list of mathematical skills each application requires for its solution. Compare your results with those of a colleague.

3. If you have a group of students at your disposal, give them several of the applications in Set 7.1. Write a short report on your observations. Compare your observations with your list of skills identified in Ex. 2.

4. A commonly used method for detecting mathematical patterns contains the following steps:
    1. *Calculate* the values of the first few elements of the sequence.
    2. *Determine* the number pattern by examining emerging number series.
    3. *Predict* values for the remaining elements by using the number pattern developed in (2).
    4. *Check* the predicted answers to these elements on your calculator or by mental arithmetic.

    Write a brief statement which addresses the educational merits of having students practice and learn this process.

7.2 Number Patterns That Teach Fundamental Concepts

Although number patterns may be used productively in the classroom for motivational and recreational purposes, a far more basic application of number patterns is in the development of fundamental concepts. It is with this process that a calculator is extremely important.

In Classroom Application Set 6.4, you explored negative numbers via sequences of ordered calculations. From the number patterns these calculations developed you were able to deduce certain rules which govern operations on negative numbers. Often by manipulating these sorts of number patterns students are able to abstract principles and gain insights they would be unable to make otherwise. Thus, because the calculator accelerates computational processes and allows students to observe emerging number patterns more quickly and accurately, operating on sequences of related exercises with calculators is a valuable strategy for teaching fundamental concepts.

But, you must take care not to "jump to conclusions" too rapidly without *checking* your predictions. Consider the following:

Calculate: $101 \times 222 =$

$101 \times 333 =$

$101 \times 444 =$

Predict: $101 \times 555 =$

Can you explain your results?

Classroom Application Set 7.2

These calculator activities are based on the four-step strategy — calculate, determine, predict, and check — presented in Exercise Set 7.1. Students should become familiar with this method and should be allowed to use it individually or in small groups. It is in these settings that students experience the joy of discovering the pattern or principle involved in each application.

1. *Developing Mental Computational Skills*
   The built-in constant multiplication function of most four-function calculators is a convenient characteristic for assisting in the development of mental computational skills. It should be applied whenever the same multiplier is used in a series of multiplication problems. Students soon realize, however, that when multiplying by 10, 100, or even 50, mental arithmetic is far more efficient than using a calculator. Activity:

   a. Calculate:
   $$6 \times 2 =$$
   $$6 \times 20 =$$
   $$6 \times 200 =$$
   $$6 \times 2,000 =$$

   State number pattern: _____

   Predict:
   $$4 \times 300 =$$
   $$4 \times 3,000 =$$

   Check

   b. Calculate:
   $$60 \times 20 =$$
   $$600 \times 200 =$$
   $$6,000 \times 20,000 =$$

   State number pattern: _____

   Predict:
   $$80 \times 40 =$$
   $$800 \times 4,000 =$$

   Check

   c. Calculate:
   $$18 \times 5 =$$
   $$18 \times 50 =$$
   $$18 \times 500 =$$
   $$18 \times 5,000 =$$

   State number pattern: _____

   Predict:
   $$24 \times 50 =$$
   $$24 \times 500 =$$
   $$24 \times 5,000 =$$

   Check

2. *Placing Decimal Points Correctly*
   Students often have difficulty with placing decimal points correctly in multiplication and division problems that involve decimal

numbers. Performing activities which develop number patterns, such as the following, can be helpful in learning these skills.

Activity:

a. Calculate:

$$2.1 \times 3.6 =$$
$$2.1 \times .36 =$$
$$2.1 \times .036 =$$
$$2.1 \times .0036 =$$

State number pattern: _____

Predict: If $4.26 \times .005 = .0213$,

find: $4.26 \times .05 =$
$$4.26 \times .5 =$$
$$4.26 \times 5 =$$

Check

Follow-up: Write three different multiplication problems for each answer. Use only the digits 0, 6, 7, and 9.

$$.096 \times .07 = .00672$$
$$\underline{\hspace{2cm}} = .00672$$
$$\underline{\hspace{2cm}} = .00672$$
$$\underline{\hspace{2cm}} = .00672$$

Check

b. Calculate:

$$12.5 \div 5 =$$
$$12.5 \div .5 =$$
$$12.5 \div .05 =$$
$$12.5 \div .005 =$$

State number pattern: _____

Predict: If $49.14 \div 7 = 7.02$,

find: $49.14 \div .7 =$
$$49.14 \div .007 =$$
$$49.14 \div .0007 =$$

Check

Follow-up: Write three different division problems for each answer. Use only the digits 0, 2, 5, and 8.

$$2.805 \div .025 = 112.2$$
$$\underline{\hspace{2cm}} = 112.2$$
$$\underline{\hspace{2cm}} = 112.2$$
$$\underline{\hspace{2cm}} = 112.2$$

Check

3. *Discovering The Meaning Of Arithmetic Operations*

The purpose of this activity is to provide students with the experience of working with multiplication as repeated addition (a building-up process) and division as repeated subtraction (a taking apart process). A modified number-pattern approach which utilizes the built-in constant function of the calculator is used for this purpose. The following activities require use of a calculator having an automatic constant for addition and for subtraction.

a. Multiplication, by definition, is a short-cut for addition. For example, 3 x 5 means that 5 is to be added three times. (Notice that adding 3, five times, also produces the same result.) To perform multiplication, such as 5 x 6, by repeated addition on your calculator, key in $\boxed{6}$ $\boxed{+}$ $\boxed{=}$ $\boxed{=}$ $\boxed{=}$ $\boxed{=}$ $\boxed{=}$. The number pattern you generate by pressing $\boxed{=}$ five times is the first five multiples of 6. Perform the following multiplication problems by repeated addition on your calculator. For each problem, give the number pattern and the answer.

i. 4 x 5	iv. 9 x 14	vii. 5 x 7.2
ii. 8 x 7	v. 21 x 13	viii. 24 x 18
iii. 12 x 11	vi. 6 x 54	ix. 16 x 3.1

Use what you know about placing decimal points in answers to multiplication problems of decimal numbers to find 1.2 x 3.9 by repeated addition. Explain how you did this problem.

b. Division can be understood as repeated subtraction. For example, 32 ÷ 8 asks: how many times can 8 be subtracted from 32? To find the answer by repeated subtraction on your calculator, key in 8 as a constant subtrahend. That is, press $\boxed{8}$ $\boxed{-}$ $\boxed{=}$. Then, key in $\boxed{3}$ $\boxed{2}$ $\boxed{=}$ $\boxed{=}$ $\boxed{=}$ $\boxed{=}$. Observe that the number 8 is subtracted four times, leaving 0. on the display screen. Thus, the answer to 32 ÷ 8 is 4. The number pattern developed by repeatedly pressing $\boxed{=}$ is a series of remainders that are generated as 8 is subtracted (24, 16, 8, 0). If a remainder appears on the display screen that is larger than zero and smaller than the subtrahend, it becomes the final fraction or a decimal as desired. For example, consider the problem 41 ÷ 3. After 3 is subtracted 13 times, the number 2 appears on the display screen. Since 3 cannot be subtracted from 2 without leaving a negative number, 2 becomes the remainder of the problem, and thus, the answer is 13⅔. Find the answers to the following division problems by repeated subtraction on your calculator. Also, give the number patterns in each case.

   i. 65 ÷ 5   iv. 697 ÷ 41   vii. 11,984 ÷ 749

  ii. 102 ÷ 17   v. 921 ÷ 102   viii. 54 ÷ 2.7

 iii. 51 ÷ 4   vi. 192.4 ÷ 26   ix. 6.9 ÷ .3

Use what you know about placing decimal points in answers to division problems of decimal numbers to find 1.09 ÷ .09 by repeated subtraction. Explain how you did this problem.

4. *Finding Decimal Names For Fractions*

Many fractions have terminating decimal names. Examples include: ½ = .5, ⅝ = .625, and ³⁄₂₀ = .15. Other fractions have decimal names which are made up of repeating digits, such as ⅑ = .$\overline{1}$, ²⁄₉₉ = .$\overline{02}$, ³⁄₄₄ = .06$\overline{81}$, and ³⁴⁄₂₇ = 1.$\overline{259}$. This activity introduces students to the repeating nature of decimal names for common fractions. It also allows students to compute and predict these decimal numbers on their calculators. Activity:

a. Calculate beginning with the column on the left.

$$\frac{1}{11} = \qquad \frac{5}{11} = \qquad \frac{23}{11} =$$

$$\frac{2}{11} = \qquad \frac{13}{11} = \qquad \frac{36}{11} =$$

$$\frac{3}{11} = \qquad \frac{16}{11} = \qquad \frac{72}{11} =$$

State number pattern: _____

Predict:

$$\frac{6}{11} = \qquad \frac{10}{11} = \qquad \frac{84}{11} =$$

$$\frac{8}{11} = \qquad \frac{59}{11} = \qquad \frac{92}{11} =$$

$$\frac{9}{11} = \qquad \frac{68}{11} = \qquad \frac{100}{11} =$$

Check

b. Calculate beginning with the column on the left.

$$\frac{1}{33} = \qquad \frac{7}{33} = \qquad \frac{37}{33} =$$

$$\frac{4}{33} = \qquad \frac{10}{33} = \qquad \frac{43}{33} =$$

State number pattern: _____

Predict:

$$\frac{5}{33} = \qquad \frac{16}{33} = \qquad \frac{53}{33} =$$

$$\frac{9}{33} = \qquad \frac{34}{33} = \qquad \frac{67}{33} =$$

Check

c. Calculate beginning with the column on the left.

$$\frac{1}{111} = \qquad \frac{10}{111} = \qquad \frac{4}{111} =$$

$$\frac{3}{111} = \qquad \frac{122}{111} = \qquad \frac{12}{333} =$$

$$\frac{5}{111} = \qquad \frac{1}{333} = \qquad \frac{337}{333} =$$

State number patterns:_____

_____

Predict:

$$\frac{2}{111} = \qquad \frac{118}{111} = \qquad \frac{15}{333} =$$

$$\frac{7}{111} = \qquad \frac{2}{333} = \qquad \frac{335}{333} =$$

$$\frac{12}{111} = \qquad \frac{10}{333} = \qquad \frac{681}{333} =$$

Check

Exercise Set 7.2

1. Work out each application in Classroom Application Set 7.2.

2. If you have a group of students at your disposal, give them several of the applications in Set 7.2. Write a short report on their ability to successfully complete these applications.

3. The intent of Classroom Application Set 7.2 is to show you how operating $(+, -, \times, \div)$ on sequences of related exercises with calculators can be a valuable strategy for teaching fundamental arithmetic concepts. With practice you will be able to create number patterns to assist you in your own teaching of basic concepts. To begin, select a topic or concept you want to teach with the assistance of number patterns. Then, make up a classroom application. If you have a group of students available, try it out on them. Write a brief paper relating your experiences. Based

on these experiences, how would you write your application differently?

4. Calculate decimal expansions for $\frac{1}{22}$ and $\frac{2}{22}$. State the number pattern. Then predict $\frac{3}{22}$. What happened? Did the decimal names for $\frac{1}{22}$ and $\frac{2}{22}$ really give you a number pattern?

5. From your experience with sequential calculations that produce number patterns and sequences of calculations that seem as if they should produce number patterns, but do not, write a brief report on the value of using number patterns as a teaching strategy in the classroom. Include both advantages and disadvantages.

7.3 Machines and Problem Solving

One approach to studying early civilizations is to study their tools. The problem of finding and preparing food was solved by use of spears, bow and arrow, fire, grinding tools, and so on. Humans have been very ingenious in recognizing particular types of problems and developing tools (machines) to aid in their solution.

The abacus was a very early aid to computation, while the electronic calculator is a quite recent invention. A study of these and other machines can make an interesting unit in a science or mathematics course.

Typically a machine is developed to help solve a specific type of problem, but has the potential to create other problems. Students can learn to look for both the advantages and disadvantages of having various machines.

Machine	Purpose	Related Problems
Telephone	Communication	Unsightly wires & poles
		Invasion of privacy
Automobile	Transportation	Environmental pollution
		Scarce resources

Classroom Application Set 7.3

These applications are designed to help lay a broad foundation for the study of machines and problem solving.

1. Divide the class into teams of two or three students. Each team is to make as long a list of types of machines as they can. Limit the time to five or ten minutes.

2. Assign students to collect pictures of different types of machines. The pictures can come from newspapers and magazines, or students can draw them. Each picture should be mounted on a 4"x6" card. Write below the picture the name of the machine and a one sentence statement of its purpose (the type of problem it is designed to help solve). Also write a sentence giving problems the machine helps add to or create.

3. Make a list of machines designed to supplement, aid, or extend the capabilities of human:

   a. Eyes
   b. Ears
   c. Legs
   d. Brain

4. Some machines can store information and/or perform a step by step set of actions automatically. Examples include an elevator and a dishwasher. Working from the machine collection (see Application 2 above), identify machines that have these character-istics. (Hopefully, students will realize that calculators and computers fall into this category.)

5. Computers and/or robots appear in many television programs, movies, and books. Make a list of those in which computers and/or robots appear. What capabilities and powers do these machines have? In what ways are they human-like? In what ways are they machine-like?

6. How smart is a computer? Discuss the meaning of the word "smart" and compare/contrast machine smartness with human smartness. (Students may believe that computers are human-like machines that are stronger and smarter than people. This indicates that their computer literacy level is low which may be largely the fault of television, movies, and comic books.)

7. Machines can be classified according to the source/nature of the energy they use. Electronic calculators and computers require electricity. Most automobiles require gasoline. For some machines, such as a crowbar, energy is supplied by human muscle. Have each student select two or three machines which have the same energy source, a source other than the user. Then, have each student write a short essay or present a short report to the class on how an energy shortage, which discontinues the use of the selected machines, would affect our society.

Exercise Set 7.3

1. If you have a group of students at your disposal, work through the applications in the previous section with them as part of a unit on machines/calculators in problem solving.

2. Make a list of the productive uses of the four-function hand-held calculator. Then, make a list of the problems associated with its use. Which of your lists is longer, more convincing? Compare your lists with those of a colleague.

3. One of the positions critics sometimes take when expressing their skepticism about the use of hand-held calculators in mathematics classrooms is that machines in general, calculators in particular, are capable, to some extent, of dictating the course of events. They believe this is dangerous. Particularly, they feel that children should not be subjected to the power of the calculator to govern the way they learn and do mathematics. Write a brief paper expressing your reaction to this statement.

4. One of the positions advocates sometimes take when expressing their arguments concerning the use of hand calculators in the classroom is that machines in general, calculators in particular, are an integral part of our society; we cannot avoid them. Thus, to prepare individuals for full participation in society, completely capable of taking advantage of the entire range of technological benefits and prepared to combat yet unforeseen technological problems, we, as adults in society, cannot afford to deprive our children from becoming completely knowledgeable about the use of machines and calculators. Write a short paper which expresses your reaction to this statement.

7.4 Representing Plans

A key aspect of problem solving is developing or deciding upon a plan. In mathematics or computer science we represent plans by written sets of directions, formulas, flow-charts, diagrams, and so on.

Each area of human endeavor has its own problems. In many cases "ordinary" English is inadequate for the precise discussion of these problems and for representing solution plans. A diagram of a football play, a cook's recipe, a pattern, a carpenter's blueprint, and a sheet of music provide diverse examples of the specialized vocabulary and notation that has developed. Often it takes considerable training and experience to learn to read, understand, and execute such plans.

Classroom Application Set 7.4

These activities are designed to help students increase their awareness of the plan-representation aspects of problem solving. Note that we tend to use the words plan and procedure interchangeably. A procedure is a detailed step-by-step set of directions designed to solve a particular type of problem.

1. Obtain some samples of music written for a piano. Explain and demonstrate to the students how the music is a detailed step-by-step set of instructions, to be interpreted and executed using a piano. If possible, let the students see a player piano in action and examine a player piano roll. (If you don't have access to a player piano, a music box will do.) Here the music is coded in a form readable by a machine, and the machine can directly interpret and execute the set of directions without human intervention. Some members of the class may enjoy reading about the history of player pianos (or music boxes) and making reports to the class.

2. Obtain some samples of knitting or weaving instructions (patterns). Explain and demonstrate to the class the relation between the instructions and the actions a human follows in executing the instructions. Bring into the discussion automatic knitting and weaving machines. Have the class suggest advantages and disadvantages of automating these processes.

3. Have each student bring a recipe to class. Discuss the idea that a recipe is a detailed step-by-step set of directions (a plan) for solving a certain type of food preparation problem. Have the students attempt to read and interpret a recipe. Discuss the abbreviations used, and the skills and knowledge that the cook is assumed to have.

4. The rules and set of directions for a game can be thought of as a plan that helps solve the problem of playing the game. Select a game that is popular with students. Obtain a set of directions. Examine and discuss with the class the relation between the set of directions and what is actually involved in playing the game well.

5. Ask students to bring to school examples of sets of directions for building or putting together things. Examples might include blueprints of house plans, instructions for assembling a bicycle or other toy, or instructions for building something using Tinkertoys or an Erector Set. Have each student explain what skills and knowledge are needed to read, interpret, and execute the set of directions they have brought to school.

6. Consider the problem students face, of getting from home to school and back. Have students represent, via writing/maps, the procedure they follow in solving this problem. One should expect considerable variations in solutions, since some students have to just walk across the school yard, while others ride a bus or other vehicle for many miles.

7. Select a place such as a museum that students can walk to from the school. Have students, working individually or in small groups, draw a detailed map giving directions on how to walk to the place. This exercise can be made more interesting by first having some of the students explain in words (no pointing) the directions for walking to the place. Then, have students compare pure oral communication with written communication, using words and maps, as a method for representing a certain type of procedure.

8. Select a game, such as Old Maid, that most students know. Divide the class into small groups, making sure each group understands the game quite well. Each group writes down a procedure, readable by students at their grade level, that can be followed by a person who does not know how to play the game. The procedure should be detailed enough so that the person following it can play the game correctly (not necessarily with the best strategy) without asking questions.

9. There is a difference between representing the rules of a game and representing the strategy to be followed to play the game well. This is illustrated by the following procedure for playing

tic-tac-toe. After students work on the two questions, (a) and (b) below, have them attempt to make up other strategies that can be followed to play the game well. Recall that in the game of tic-tac-toe, two players alternately take turns placing a mark (X for one player, O for the other) onto a 3 x 3 grid. The first player to get three marks in a row, column or diagonal wins. A row, column, or diagonal is called a file. Suppose the squares of the board are numbered as follows:

2	6	3
7	1	8
4	9	5

Consider the following procedure to be used by player X for making a move:

i. If there is a file containing two X's and no O's, play in that file. (If two such moves exist, make the one that involves the lowest numbered square.) Otherwise:

ii. If there is a file with two O's and no X's, play in that file. (If two such moves exist, make the one that involves the the lowest numbered square.) Otherwise:

iii. If there is any move that will create two files, each containing two X's and no O's, make that move. (If two such moves exist, make the one that involves the lowest numbered square.) Otherwise:

iv. Play in the unused square of lowest number.

a. Let X play first. Determine whether or not X can be beaten by player O.

b. Suppose O is allowed to play first, while X follows the above procedure; now answer (a).

10. Clerks in stores and other people learn procedures for making change. Thus, if you purchase something costing $.23 and hand the clerk a dollar bill, the clerk may hand you the item, saying "$.23." Next, the clerk hands you two pennies, saying "and 2 makes twenty-five cents." Finally the clerk hands you 3 quarters saying "$.50, $.75, and another quarter makes one dollar." Using play money (or real), have members of the class, working in teams of two, practice making change. Then have each team write down a change-making procedure. The problem can be simplified by limiting the amount of the purchase to one dollar or less, and the amount of money tendered to be exactly one dollar. Or, one can make the problem more difficult by allowing the size of the purchase, and the amount tendered, to be any amount. In all cases, the change is to be made using the smallest possible number of coins. In the example at the beginning of this application, it was assumed that no half dollars were available.

11. This activity assumes that students know how to write the Roman numerals from 1 to 20 (I to XX). To begin, have each student write the Roman numerals from I to XX. Then give the students some addition problems in which each of the two addends is X or less. Finally, have each student write down a procedure that can be followed to add any

two Roman numerals of value X or less. After these procedures have been written down, have class members exchange papers and attempt to follow each other's procedures.

A flowchart can be used to represent a procedure. Students can learn to read and follow the directions in a flowchart. Doing so exposes them to ideas of flowcharting and gives them practice in following detailed sets of directions. The next four activities are based upon the following flowchart.

12. Follow the flowchart and record the resulting value of C.

a. A = 4   d. A = 7
b. A = 3   e. A = 289
c. A = 8   f. A = 5280

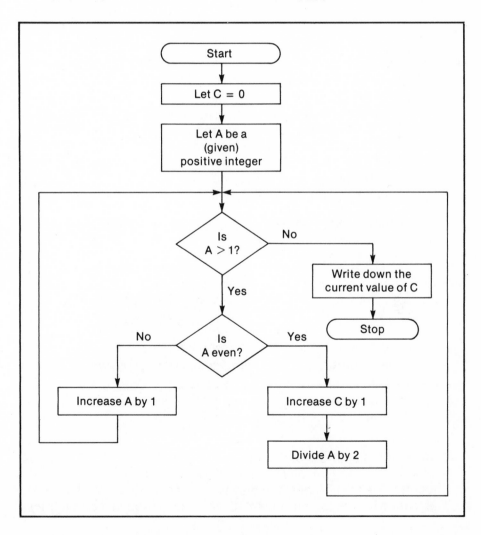

13. Figure out a value for A so that the resulting value for C will be as follows.

    a. C = 2   b. C = 5   c. C = 10   d. C = 20

14. After completing 13 above, find another (different) solution to each of the four questions in application 13.

15. Change the flowchart so that the box containing "Increase A by 1" is replaced by a box which reads "Increase A by 1 and decrease C by 1." Then, solve 12, 13, and 14 again.

Exercise Set 7.4

1. Devising plans to solve problems lies at the heart of the problem-solving process. It often is the most difficult, and at the same time, the most rewarding of the five problem-solving steps (see chapter 3). Students learn how to acquire solution plans by observing how others solve problems and by practicing these methods. The applications in the previous set provide a wide variety of experiences in which students can observe and devise problem-solving procedures. Examine each application carefully. Then, write a brief statement (two or three sentences) for each application, which identifies the instructional purpose of the application and the method by which this purpose is achieved.

2. If you have a group of students available, select at least five of the applications from the previous set that are appropriate for their ability level and which seem to fit well together as an instructional unit. Present this unit to your students. From your observations of this activity, write a brief paper which relates:

    a. Students' interest in and enthusiasm for the lesson.

    b. Their ability to achieve the purposes of the lesson.

    c. Their ability to abstract certain general problem-solving procedures from the lesson. (Identify them.)

3. Many of the applications contained in Set 7.4 deal with situations which are not typically found in most mathematics curricula. Identify the advantages and disadvantages of incorporating these activities into regular problem-solving instruction in mathematics.

7.5 Problems With Large Numbers

To a first grader a number such as 897 seems quite large. To a teacher with a monthly take-home pay of $897 it doesn't seem so large. Part of math education is to help students develop an intuitive understanding, a "feel," for the meaning of numbers of various sizes. A calculator is a useful aid in this endeavor.

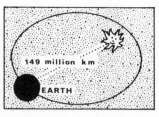

Large numbers do occur naturally. For example, the speed of light in a vacuum is stated as 186,000 miles per second, and distances to stars are stated as numbers of light years. A light year is approximately:

186,000 miles/second × 365 days/year × 24 hrs/day
× 60 min/hr × 60 sec/min

The product 186,000 × 365 × 24 × 60 × 60 will overflow an eight-digit calculator. But, we can use a calculator to find 186 × 365 × 24 × 6 × 6 = 58,656,960. Thus, we conclude the answer is approximately 5,865,696,000,000 miles. This is an approximation since 186,000 is correct to only three digits and 365 is correct to only three digits. A scientist might state the result as 5,870,000,000,000 miles or 5.87×10^{12} miles or 5.9×10^{12} miles.

In working with large numbers one is often forced to keep track of powers of 10. Also, one should realize that often only the first few digits are significant. One does not obtain eight-significant-digit accuracy when working with three-significant-digit measurements.

Classroom Application Set 7.5

These activities are designed to give students practice in solving problems with large numbers.

1. Suppose there are 24 students in a class. Each school day each student brings a penny and gives it to the teacher. At the end of the 180-day school year how many pennies will the teacher have? Is this enough to buy a new car?

2. The distance across the United States is about 5,000 km. Suppose that a person can walk 3 km/hr and 8 hours per day. How many days would it take to walk across the country? Suppose a car is driven at 85 km/hr for 8 hours per day. How many days will it take for it to cross the country?

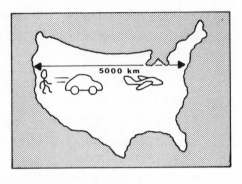

3. What is your age in years? In months? In hours? In seconds?

4. In a classic story a servant performs a good deed for the king. The king asks what reward the servant would like. The servant requests one grain of wheat for the first square on a chess board, 2 grains for the second, 4 grains for the third, 8 grains for the fourth, etc. There are 64 squares on a chess board. Find approximate values for the number of grains the servant is requesting for the 64th square and for the total.

5. A factory worker is paid $7.85 per hour. If the worker works 8 hours per day, five days per week, 52 weeks per year, for 40 years, what will the total pay be?

6. A recent Rose Bowl football game was attended by 104,000 people. Suppose the average person attending had a mass of 67kg and a height of 162 cm.

   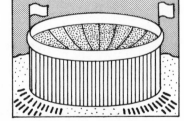

   a. What was the total mass of the people?
   b. What was the total height of the people?
   c. If the people were laid end to end would they stretch across your state in an east-west direction?

7. A particular novel has about 12 words per line, 58 lines per page, and 375 pages. How long will it take to read this novel if one can read 260 words per minute?

8. The earth is about 400,000 km from the moon and 149,000,000 km from the sun. How long would it take to drive each of these distances at a speed of 85 km/hr, driving 8 hours per day?

9. Class projects: Estimate

a. The total number of words in all of the books in your classroom.
b. The total number of words in all of the books in your school library.
c. The average number of letters per word in the books in your classroom and your school library.

10. Individual projects: Estimate
    a. The number of times your heart beats in a year.
    b. The number of breaths you take in a year.
    c. The number of hours you watch television in a year.
    d. The number of hours you spend eating in a year.
    e. The number of hours you spend in school in a year.
    f. The number of hours you spend sleeping in a year.
    g. The number of words you read in a year.
    h. The number of words you speak in a year.

Exercise Set 7.5

1. Find solutions to each of the applications in this section. Place each at an appropriate grade-level range (that is, grades 3-5, grades 7-8, etc.). Then explain how you would use them in your teaching.

2. For the grade level at which you teach or plan to teach make a list of mathematical topics for which the inclusion of problems with large numbers seems appropriate. Then examine a standard mathematics textbook written for this level and determine whether it provides discussion and exercises with large numbers for the topics in your list. What value do you see in students solving problems with large numbers?

3. Identify areas of the school curriculum, other than mathematics, that can be explored or supplemented by students solving problems with large numbers.

7.6 The Calculator and the School Curriculum

Calculator usage is now commonplace in the home and in business. The calculator is slowly but irresistibly invading the elementary and middle school curriculum. It is inevitible that this invasion be slow, since it involves the development of new materials, extensive teacher training, and modification of well established habits.

By the 1990's use of calculators in the elementary and middle school will be commonplace, and calculators will have contributed to a significant change in the mathematics curriculum. While predicting the future is difficult, we suggest that the following will occur:

1. There will be less time devoted to the acquisition of pencil and paper computational skills. The current emphasis upon memorizing single digit arithmetic facts will continue, and there will be increased emphasis upon mental arithmetic.

2. Greater emphasis will be placed upon problem solving, both directly in mathematics and in fields using math as a tool. The problems to be studied will be more interdisciplinary and real world in nature.

3. More time will be spent studying and practicing general techniques of problem solving. Techniques such as guess and check, or exhaustive search of all possible solutions (which may make use of a calculator or a computer) will be taught.

4. There will be an increased emphasis upon understanding the general idea of algorithm, and of developing and representing algorithms.

5. The combination of increased use of the metric system and increased use of calculators will lead to the earlier introduction of decimals and a decreased emphasis upon calculation with fractions. But fractions will remain as an important part of the mathematics curriculum.

6. There will be a rapid increase in the availability and use of computers (see chapter 8).

The possible effects upon students of these changes to the school curriculum could, indeed, be dramatic. Students may well become more productive and creative problem solvers, owing to the facts that problem solving will become a more important part of the curriculum and the problems students solve will relate more significantly to their daily lives. Students could develop a better understanding of and facility with the real number system. And, finally, students at all. abilities levels could find mathematics more enjoyable and relevant to their needs, and thus, become able to apply the skills they learn to other topics in the curriculum.

Exercise Set 7.6

1. Either individually or with a colleague, develop a brief questionnaire for the purpose of assessing attitudes regarding the role of calculators in the school curriculum.

2. Administer your questionnaire (Ex 1) to two of the following groups:
   a. Colleagues
   b. Students
   c. School principals
   d. Parents

   Give a brief report of your questionnaire and findings to your class, or otherwise make copies of your findings available to your colleagues.

EIGHT
Calculators and
Computers

As you have seen, four-function electronic calculator is a marvelous aid to problem solving. But, it can be improved to make it still more useful. We have looked at two types of enhancements. The addition of more memory allows one to store intermediate answers while performing computations on other numbers. The addition of more function keys makes problems such as $\sqrt{x}$, $1/x$, x^2, x^y into primitives.

Some additional ways to improve a calculator are:

- Improve the output display. For example, this can be done by adding a printer.

- Increase the accuracy to 10 or 12 digits and add scientific notation.

- Make the machine programmable.

- Greatly increase the size of memory and provide for storage of programs or data outside of the calculator.

We begin by focusing upon the latter two points. This will provide a natural lead into computers, which we will discuss briefly. We conclude this chapter with a brief introduction to computers in education.

8.1 Repetition

There are many computational situations in which the same general task must be performed over and over again. Calculating a payroll is an example. For each worker one adds up the hours worked; multiplies by the rate of pay; and determines deductions for insurance, state taxes, federal taxes, and social security, etc.

Teachers encounter repetition when they add up test scores or determine grades. Consider the following problem:

Suppose that you have given three tests to a class. You wish to determine a weighted average score for each student, based 25% on the first test, 33% on the second test, and 42% on the third test.

As usual, the first task is to understand the problem. Suppose a student has test scores of 85, 75, and 90. Then the student's weighted average score is .25 × 85 + .33 × 75 + .42 × 90, which is 83.8.

Next, suppose that our goal is to give a procedure to be carried out by a person equipped with a simple four-function calculator, paper, and pencil. For convenience in discussing this problem, let us designate a student's three test scores by the names S1, S2, and S3 respectively. In the problem above, S1 is 85, S2 is 75, and S3 is 90. Since the scores vary for different students, it is desirable to treat them as variables. A procedure for solving the problem is given below.

1. Select a student whose weighted average has not yet been computed.

2. Read the student's first test score, S1. Using the calculator, compute .25 × S1. Record the answer on a sheet of scratch paper.

3. Read the student's second test score, S2. Using the calculator, compute .33 × S2. Record the answer on a sheet of scratch paper.

4. Read the student's third test score, S3. Using the calculator, compute .42 × S3.

5. Add to the result in step 4 the first of the two numbers recorded on the scratch paper for this student.

6. Add to the result of step 5 the second of the two numbers recorded on the scratch paper for this student. Round this result to one decimal place and record it in the gradebook, as the student's weighted average.

7. Have all students' weighted averages been computed? If "no", go to step 1. Otherwise stop.

Try this procedure on the set of data given below. Do not use the "extra" memory features of your calculator, such as a four-key memory system.

Sally Brown   87 92 58

Don Jones   79 83 67

Terry Walker   63 98 86

You will find that this is a lot of work!

The procedure illustrates inadequacies of the simple calculator. For each student the multipliers .25, .33, and .42 must be keyed in. For each student the intermediate results .25 × S1 and .33 × S2 must be written on scratch paper. Later these numbers must be keyed into the calculator, to add to the value .42 × S3.

The use of a four-key memory system makes the calculation simpler. The intermediate results .25 × S1 and .33 × S2 are added to memory rather than written on scratch paper. Still, the multipliers .25, .33, and .42 must be keyed in for each student. A programmable calculator has enough memory to remove this last difficulty.

If a programmable calculator has been properly programmed, then the steps needed to compute a student's weighted average would be as follows:

1. Depress the "Continue" key.
2. Key in the value S1 and depress the "Continue" key.
3. Key in the value S2 and depress the "Continue" key.
4. Key in the value S3 and depress the "Continue" key.
5. Read the answer displayed by the calculator, round it to one decimal place, and record it in the gradebook.
6. If all students have not yet been processed, go to step 1. Otherwise stop.

It should be evident that a person equipped with a properly programmed programmable calculator could process a classes' scores about twice as fast as a person using just a simple four-function calculator with four-key memory. The key to this is the programmable calculator and its program.

A program is a step-by-step set of directions written in a form that is "understandable" to the machine. A programmable calculator can store such a set of directions, and then execute them. The actual process of entering a program into a programmable calculator is simple. One merely depresses a sequence of keys which corresponds to the steps in the program.

A program for the weighted average problem could be as follows:

1. Wait until directed to 'Continue'.
2. Accept a number (that is, S1) to be keyed in.
3. Multiply it by .25 and store the result in a memory location M.
4. Accept a number (that is, S2) to be keyed in.
5. Multiply it by .33, add the number in memory location M, and store the result in memory location M. This erases the old contents of M.
6. Accept a number (that is, S3) to be keyed in.
7. Multiply it by .42 and add the result to the number in memory location M. Display (that is, output) the result.
8. Go to step 1.

Exercise Set 8.1

1. Make a list of repetitive computational tasks that occur in business, science, or everyday life.
2. A teacher has given five tests to a class of students. They are to be weighted 20%, 15%, 25%, 10%, and 30% respectively. Write a detailed set of instructions on how to carry out the computation using a four-function calculator, and then using a four-function calculator with memory. Make up a sample set of data for three students and process it using each of your sets of instructions.

3.

A certain bank pays 6% interest compounded quarterly. That is, 1½% interest is added on at the end of each three month period. A person deposits $1,000 at the beginning of each quarter for three years, a total of 12 deposits. How much will the person have at the end of three years?

Complete the table, rounding each amount to the nearest cent.

DATE	DEPOSIT	INTEREST	BALANCE
1 January 1981	$1,000.00	— —	$1,000.00
1 April 1981	$1,000.00	$15.00	$2,015.00
1 July 1981	$1,000.00	$30.22	$3,045.22
1 October 1981	$1,000.00	$45.68	_____
1 January 1982	$1,000.00	_____	_____
1 April 1982	_____	_____	_____
1 July 1982	_____	_____	_____
1 October 1982	_____	_____	_____
1 January 1983	_____	_____	_____
1 April 1983	_____	_____	_____
1 July 1983	_____	_____	_____
1 October 1983	_____	_____	_____

8.2 Programmable Calculators

A programmable calculator has a memory large enough to store a detailed step-by-step set of directions. It can also store a considerable number of intermediate results. Finally, it can automatically follow a set of directions stored in its memory.

The size of memory in a programmable calculator varies with the cost of the machine and how recently it was designed and manufactured. Early programmable calculators were limited to programs of a few dozen steps in length. But, the circuitry used in calculator and computer memory has become smaller and cheaper. Now a hand-held calculator may have enough memory to store a thousand-step program and hundreds of intermediate answers simultaneously!

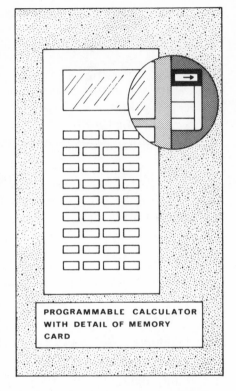

PROGRAMMABLE CALCULATOR WITH DETAIL OF MEMORY CARD

Another key feature of a programmable calculator is its capability to use external memory. This type of memory is recorded on magnetic cards or magnetic strips and stored outside of the machine. A card or strip is coated with the same type of material used to make tape recorder tape. The calculator contains a reading and writing mechanism, much like a miniature tape recorder. This mechanism can read programs that have been recorded on a magnetic card or strip and store them in the calculator memory. It can also write the contents of calculator memory onto a card or strip.

A second way programmable calculators are able to access external memory is through the use of plug-in units of memory that contain built-in program. The programs in these units are permanently stored and cannot be changed or erased by the user. Thus, they are similar in nature to the built-in functions of multi-function calculators.

The idea of plug-in memory has proven very successful. A manufacturer designs libraries of programs of interest to specific groups of people. One library may solve surveying problems; a second may solve navigational problems; a third may provide drill and practice in arithmetic facts. Users purchase only the program libraries they need, along with basic programmable calculators.

Once a program is developed, it can be stored. Programs are often stored on paper in a written form. But this method of program storage entails keying in the program each time it is used. A much more convenient method is to use magnetic cards or strips, or plug-in units. These approaches to program storage make programs that are hundreds of steps long rapidly accessible.

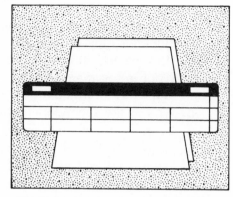

Previously, we commented on how a calculator gives a person an increased set of primitives. Square root is available at the touch of a key. A multi-function calculator may contain as many as 50 to 100 built-in functions. But, a program library for a programmable calculator is not limited in size. It may contain many thousands of programs, and more can be added in the future. Needless to say, this has the potential of causing a significant change in mathematics education and in the disciplines making extensive use of mathematics.

From time to time people have experimented with the use of programmable calculators in elementary and middle schools. Students can learn to use programs from a program library. Also, they can learn to construct simple programs.

By and large, however, use of programmable calculators does not seem particularly suited to this level. First, such calculators contain a large number of built-in functions, such as SIN, COS, TAN, LOG, EXP, etc., which are completely beyond the mathematical level of the students. Second, students at this level have a few problems or interests that require such sophisticated calculation. A student can learn to write a factorial program. (n!, read "n factorial," is defined by n! = 1 × 2 × 3 × . . . n.) But, this does not solve a problem that ordinarily appears in the elementary or middle school curriculum.

Also, computers are now cheap enough to provide a viable alternative. If a student is going to learn to program, why not learn to program a computer? A hand-held, battery powered computer, programmable in the language BASIC, is now available for about $150.

Exercise Set 8.2

1. Go to a store that sells programmable calculators, or in some other manner examine several of them. Answer the following questions:

   a. Which brands use RPN (reverse Polish notation) and which use algebraic logic?

   b. How many built-in functions does each machine have?

   c. What is the memory size in terms of the number of program steps and intermediate answers or data that can be stored?

   d. What is the secondary memory (magnetic card, magnetic strip, plug-in unit, etc.)?

   e. What is the nature and extent of available libraries of programs?

   f. What is the range of prices?

2. If Ex. 1 is done at a store, ask the clerk to show you how to write a simple program and enter it into one of the calculators. Likely the clerk will not have this level of skill or knowledge. Discuss this situation, relating your discussion to our educational system.

8.3 Computers

There is no clear dividing line between calculators and computers. As one adds more and more capabilities to a calculator when does it become a computer?

Still, it is convenient to distinguish computers from calculators by three major characteristics.

1. Computers work with a character set consisting of digits, *letters*, and most of the rest of the special characters found on a typewriter. A machine which is "purely" a calculator works only with numbers.

2. Computers are much faster than calculators. A relatively inexpensive computer is apt to be a hundred times as fast as an expensive programmable calculator, although they may cost the same.

3. Computers are programmable in "higher-level languages" such as BASIC, COBOL, LOGO, or PASCAL (more on this later). The typical programmable calculator is programmed in a less sophisticated language.

A computer is a machine consisting of hardware (physical machinery) and software (computer programs). A computer cannot function usefully without programs. These may be written in the language the machine was wired (constructed) to understand, called machine language. Or, they may be written in a more human-like language created by humans and useful on a wide variety of different brands of computers. These high-level languages have names such as BASIC, COBOL, LOGO, and PASCAL. Humans write programs in these languages and computer programs are used to translate from the higher-level language programs into machine language. These translating programs are thousands of instructions long, and may require several years of effort to develop. A different translator is needed for each programming language. Also, a different translator is needed for each different computer model.

If one ignores the issue of software, then a computer can be thought of as a superspeed programmable calculator that uses an electric typewriter for input and output. A more sophisticated model of computer hardware is provided by the diagram below.

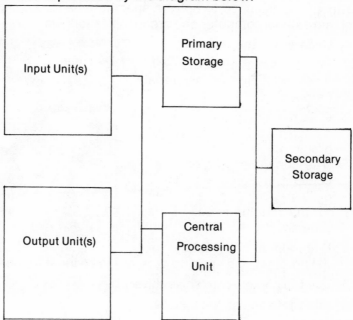

The following represent various computer hardware units.

Input Units: Keyboard terminal (like a typewriter)
 Card reader
 Optical scanner

Output Units: Keyboard terminal with printer or TV-like display
 Line printer
 Plotter

Central Processing Unit: Contains the circuitry to interpret and automatically carry out a step-by-step set of directions (a program) in primary storage.

Primary Storage: Temporary storage space for programs and data being worked on by the CPU. This is like the memory in a calculator.

Secondary Storage: Magnetic tape, magnetic discs, bubble memory, and other media for the permanent or temporary storage of large amounts of data and programs.

A computer program is a plan, a detailed step-by-step set of instructions, designed to solve a specific type of problem. To solve a problem using a computer one proceeds as follows:

1. Understand the problem.
2. Decide that a computer will be a useful aid in solving the problem.
3. Obtain a computer program designed to solve this type of problem.
(The computer program may come from a program library, or it may have to be written for the specific needs of the problem.)

4. Understand how details of the problem, and specific data, are to be input to the computer.
5. Use the computer to solve the problem.
6. Interpret and use the results.

These steps are quite similar to the general plan for problem solving you studied earlier in this book. A computer is merely an automated plan-executor. It can execute very complicated plans very rapidly. An inexpensive computer may execute 10,000 program steps per second, while an expensive computer may execute 10,000,000 program steps per second.

The essence of computer science is developing ways of representing problems and data, and developing programs to solve problems. The beginnings of these skills can be taught in elementary school.

Exercise Set 8.3

1. Estimate how long it takes you to find the product of two four-digit numbers by hand and by calculator. Then, estimate how long it would take you to do 10 million of these multiplication problems by each method.

2. Select a recent issue of *The Arithmetic Teacher* and page through it. How many of the ads and articles mention calculators or computers? Compute the percentages involved.

3. Select several other publications aimed at elementary teachers and page through them. How many ads and articles about calculators and computers are in these publications? Compute the percentages involved.

4. Some companies which are prominent in the computer field include International Business Machines, Honeywell, Sperry, Digital Equipment, Control Data, Tandy, Apple, Commodore, Texas Instruments, and Atari. Select one of these Companies and study the range of computer products sold and how these products are used in education.

8.4 Microcomputers

Complete computer systems range in price from about $500 to $12 million. Those near the bottom end of the scale are called micro-computers. The name comes not from the low price, but from the circuitry used in the central processing unit. It is now possible to construct a 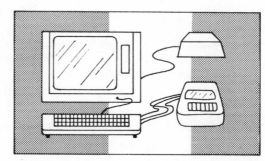 single large-scale integrated circuit, less than one centimetre on a side, which contains all of the circuitry of a CPU. This is called a microprocessor. A computer whose CPU is a microprocessor is called a microcomputer.

A modern microcomputer contains enough primary storage so that it can use languages such as BASIC, COBOL, LOGO, or PASCAL. Typically the computer comes equipped with a BASIC translator already (and permanently) stored in part of its primary memory. Additional software, such as a COBOL, LOGO, or PASCAL translator, costs extra.

Even the least expensive microcomputer can be a useful educational tool in the hands of an appropriately trained teacher. But, such a machine is severely limited in overall usefulness. An inexpensive microcomputer uses a TV set for output display. This display is of modest visual quality and provides no permanent printed copy. Printed output is *very* important in many educational applications.

An inexpensive microcomputer uses a cassette tape recorder for secondary storage. It may take several minutes to read a program into

primary storage, or to copy a program from primary storage onto tape. The tape systems are finicky, prone to error, and a major source of frustration to computer users.

An inexpensive microcomputer has a relatively small primary storage and relatively slow speed. This restricts the nature of the programs it can handle.

In spite of these problems a microcomputer is a versatile and useful aid to instruction. Since the lowest price is about the same as a color television set, a microcomputer can easily be afforded by most elementary and middle schools. Whether a school decides to purchase a microcomputer should be based upon how it will be used.

8.5 Computers In Education

As with calculators, it is convenient to divide the computers in education field into three parts.

- Teaching about computers.
- Teaching using computers.
- Impact upon the curriculum.

Teaching about computers requires teacher knowledge. It makes no sense for a school to acquire computers for this purpose unless it also commits itself to a teacher training program. The depth of the necessary training is subject to debate. However, minimally the equivalent of a three-credit college course is needed to give a basic understanding of computers. Several additional courses, or substantial self-instruction, are needed before one should begin teaching computer programming.

Teaching using computers requires only a modest amount of teacher knowledge and experience. The key to this is having an adequate library of appropriate computer programs. The supply of educational software is growing rapidly. But, deciding upon appropriate software, and acquiring it, is a time consuming and expensive process. It should not be undertaken lightly. Nor, is it an appropriate task for a teacher with very little or no training and experience in the computer field.

Computers will eventually have a major impact upon the curriculum. Students will learn to use computers, in the same way they now use complicated devices such as television sets, telephones, tape recorders, and electric typewriters. Teaching using computers will become common both at school and in the home.

Computers will also affect what is taught. We have touched upon this with calculators and mathematics. The ready availability of calculators changes what is worthwhile to learn, or what it means to "know" something. So it is with computers, but in a wider variety of disciplines. One can gain some insight into this by looking at the variety of activities that are undertaken by computer scientists.

8.6 Computer Science

The essence of computer science is the study of problem solving using computers. As the field has matured many subfields have developed. A computer scientist may well specialize in one of these subfields, spending many hours each day grappling with its problems.

Information Retrieval: A singal modern disk pack, about 35 cm in diameter and 15 cm high, can store the equivalent of a thousand full length novels or thick textbooks. A computer can access any piece of this material in a fraction of a second. There now exists computerized storage devices that can store a million volume library. The study of the computerized storage and retrieval of information is called information retrieval.

An important part of our current education is learning how to "look up" information. We learn to use a dictionary, encyclopedia, telephone book, and library. Students of the future will also learn to use a computer for such purposes. The nature of libraries will change significantly.

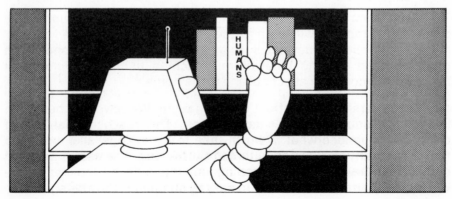

Computer Graphics: An ancient Chinese proverb states that a picture is worth more than 10,000 words. A computer can store and manipulate electronic representations of pictures, such as a television picture. It can also store numbers representing graphs, charts, engineering or architectural drawings, and so on. The computer can output pictures as line drawings on a plotter, which may have several different colors of pens. Or it may output a picture to a television-like display, which may be black and white or color. A computer

may output using a xerox-like process, again using black and white or color.

Computer graphics has become an essential tool of many scientists, engineers, architects, and science fiction movie makers. With appropriate hardware and software very young children can display their artistic skills and experience considerable satisfaction, while learning about computer graphics. The cost of such facilities has decreased rapidly in recent years, and is not within reach of schools. Microcomputer systems which use a color television set for output, and which offer quite good computer graphics facilities, are now available.

Computer Music: A tone generator, which plays a single note at a time, adds perhaps $10 to the cost of a microcomputer. Such a computer can be programmed to play tunes that sound much like a child produces while playing the piano with one finger. For about $500 one can equip a microcomputer with a music generator that generates a half dozen tones simultaneously. This is roughly equivalent to being able to play up to six simultaneous notes on a piano. Very high quality music can be programmed into the computer and played by such an output device.

Computerized music is now fairly common. There is a widely circulated journal on computer music. Many college and university music departments use computers in ear training. The use as an aid to composition training is now catching on.

At the grade school level it is easy to imagine a child being able to create beautiful and expressive music. Now a child can create music at a computer keyboard and the computer can perform it.

Computer Simulation: You are very used to using mathematical models while problem solving, although you may not realize it. If a problem involves Terry having six marbles, you use the mathematical symbol 6 to represent the situation. The 6 is a mathematical model for Terry's marbles.

Similarly, a formula such as $A = lw$ is a mathematical model of certain aspects of a rectangle. Other models, such as $D = RT$ and $E = mc^2$, are also commonplace.

A computerized model, using a computer program to represent the model and a computer to carry out calculations it specifies, is called a computer simulation. Since modeling and simulation are fundamental to all sciences, computer simulation is a very widely applicable discipline. For example, a city planner may make use of a computer model of the street plan and traffic flow in a city.

Because modeling and simulation are at the very heart of all sciences, one would think that these

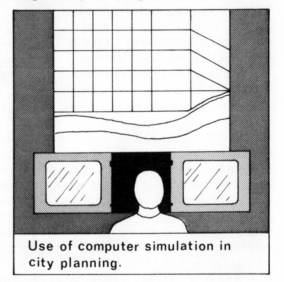

Use of computer simulation in city planning.

ideas would be introduced in the elementary school, or certainly in secondary school. The computer, and computer simulation, provide an extra motivation for doing so. Students can make use of computer simulations as an aid to learning about the physical system being modeled.

Also, it is interesting to think about computer assisted instruction (CAI) in light of simulation. In CAI, a computer is taking over some of the functions of a teacher. That is, CAI is a computer simulation of certain aspects of teaching.

Artificial Intelligence: How smart is a computer? In some ways the question doesn't make any sense at all, since smartness refers to people, and perhaps to certain animals. But, a calculator with a $\sqrt{}$ key can automatically calculate a square root. It takes a human many hours of studying and practice to learn to perform this task. In this sense the calculator has some "artificial intelligence."

Computers have been programmed to play checkers and chess, do medical diagnostic work, and even carry on a written conversation. They can solve complicated logic puzzles, and even solve "story" problems from algebra and calculus.

Whether or not you choose to call this intelligence, you must admit that artificial intelligence has the potential of changing education drastically. What should humans learn to do:

- mentally?
- assisted by books?
- assisted by pencil and paper?
- assisted by calculators or computers?

Suppose a computerized machine can read EEG, EKG, X-ray, or other medical test information just as well as a well trained doctor. There are many things for a doctor to learn, and no doctor can possibly keep up with all of the new results in the field. Should a medical school spend time training a doctor to do things by hand (mentally, using paper and pencil) that a machine can do?

This educational question does not have a simple answer. But, more and more of the problems we teach students to solve can also be solved by a computer. As computers become more capable we need to continually ask: What should we expect students to learn?

Other Aspects of Computer Science: We have by no means covered all of the major subfields of computer science. The design of computer circuitry is now a standard part of all electrical engineering curricula. Indeed, many engineering colleges offer a computer science degree program through their electrical engineering departments.

Numerical analysis is the branch of computer science that deals with solving math problems on a computer. It includes such topics as study of the calculator (and computer) number system, rounding or truncation errors in calculation, calculation of functions such as $\sqrt{}$ and x^y, and solution of complicated mathematical equations.

Languages such as BASIC, COBOL, LOGO, and PASCAL are created by humans. The design and implementation of new programming languages is an important part of computer science. How does one design a language that is well suited to solving problems, easy for humans to learn, and appropriate for use on a computer? Progress in this field leads to the development of new and better languages.

Business data processing is often recognized as a subfield of computer science. Perhaps 75% of all general purpose computer usage is closely tied to business. Here computers are used for inventory control, customer records, accounting, billing, planning, information retrieval, and word processing. The latter refers to computerizing a typewriter to increase its versatility and its user's productivity.

Exercise Set 8.6

1. What should we expect students to learn? Discuss this question in light of calculator and computer technology, as well as other changes in our society and technology.

8.7 Last Words

The fields of calculator education and computer education are in their infancy. We do not yet know whether a monster has been spawned, or whether these fields will prove especially beneficial to humans. In many ways we are in a situation similar to the invention of reading and writing, or the invention of the printing press. The technology exists and it will be used.

The key to "good" use lies with an informed citizenry. Educated, intelligent, well-meaning people must make the decisions. Teachers and other educators will play an important role in the decision making, and are critical to implementing changes to education. Thus, it is people like you who must become knowledgeable about calculators and computers in education.

Reading a book like this helps. But, learning by doing — trying out ideas in the classroom — is even more important. Now that you have studied this book, you know enough to begin using calculators in the classroom.

This decision to make use of your newly acquired knowledge should be backed up by a decision to learn more about calculators and computers in education. An excellent source of information is *The Computing Teacher*, a journal for educators. The main emphasis of the journal is upon educational use of calculators and computers at the pre-college level and upon teacher education.

The Computing Teacher
David Moursund, Editor
Dept. of Computer & Information Science
University of Oregon
Eugene, Oregon 97403

REFERENCE LIST

Advani, K. *The effect of the use of desk calculators on achievement and attitude of children with learning and behavior problems — A research report.* Toronto: Ontario Educational Research Council, 1972. (ERIC Document Reproduction Service No. 077 160)

Andersen, L.E. The effects of using restricted and unrestricted modes of representation with electronic calculators on the achievement and attitude of seventh grade pupils (Doctoral dissertation, University of Denver, 1976). *Dissertation Abstracts International*, 1977, *37*, 6321A-6322A. (University Microfilms No. 77-7, 399)

Bell, M., Esty, E., Payne, J.N., & Suydam, M.N. Hand-held calculators: Past, present, and future. In F. J. Crosswhite (Ed.), *Organizing for mathematics instruction* (1977 NCTM Yearbook). Reston, Virginia: National Council of Teachers of Mathematics, 1977.

Betts, E. A. A preliminary investigation of the value of a calculating machine for arithmetic instruction. *Education*, 1937, *58*, 229-235.

Boling, M.A.N. Some cognitive and affective aspects of the use of hand-held calculators in high school consumer mathematics classes (Doctoral Dissertation, The Louisiana State University and Agricultural and Mechanical College, 1977). *Dissertation Abstracts International*, 1977, *38*, 2623A-2624A. (University Microfilms No. 77-25, 370)

Borden. V. L. Teaching decimal concepts to sixth grade students using the hand-held calculator (Doctoral dissertation, University of Northern Colorado, 1976). *Dissertation Abstracts International*, 1977, *37*, 4192A. (University Microfilms No. 76-29, 734)

Cech, J. P. The effect of the use of desk calculators on attitude and achievement with low-achieving ninth graders. *Mathematics Teacher*, 1972, *65*, 183-186.

Durrance, V. R. The effect of the rotary calculator on arithmetic achievement in grades six, seven, and eight (Doctoral dissertation, George Peabody College for Teachers, 1964). *Dissertation Abstracts*, 1965, *25*, 6307. (University Microfilms No. 65-3, 541)

Fehr, H. F., McMeen, G., & Sobel, M. Using hand-operated computing machines in learning arithmetic. *Arithmetic Teacher*, 1956, *3*, 145-150.

Gaslin, W. L. A comparison of achievement and attitudes of students using conventional or calculator-based algorithms for operations on positive rational numbers in ninth-grade general mathematics. *Journal for Research in Mathematics Education*, 1975, *6*, 95-108.

Hawthorne, F. S. Hand-held calculator: Help or hindrance? *Arithmetic Teacher*, 1973, *20*, 671-672.

Hawthorne, F. S., & Sullivan, J. J. Using hand-held calculators in sixth-grade mathematics lessons. *New York State Mathematics Teachers' Journal*, 1975, *25*(1), 29-31.

Hutton, L. A. W. The effects of the use of mini-calculators on attitude and achievement in mathematics (Doctoral dissertation, Indiana University, 1976). *Dissertation Abstracts International*, 1977, *37*, 4934A. (University Microfilms No. 77-3, 347)

Jones, E. W. The effect of the hand-held calculator on mathematics achievement, attitude and self concept of sixth grade students (Doctoral dissertation, Virginia Polytechnic Institute and State University, 1976). *Dissertation Abstracts International*, 1976, *37*, 1387A. (University Microfilms No. 76-19, 885)

Machlowitz, E. Electronic calculators — Friend or foe of instruction? *Mathematics Teacher*, 1976, *69*, 104-106.

Mastbaum, S. A study of the relative effectiveness of electric calculators or computation skill kits in the teaching of mathematics (Doctoral dissertation, University of Minnesota, 1969). *Dissertation Abstracts International*, 1969, *30*, 2422A-2423A. (University Microfilms No. 69-20,036)

National Advisory Committee on Mathematical Education. *Overview and analysis of school mathematics grades K-12.* Reston, Virginia: National Council of Teachers of Mathematics, 1975.

NCTM Instructional Affairs Committee. Minicalculators in schools. *Arithmetic Teacher*, 1976, *23*, 72-74.

Nelson, D. W. Effects of using hand calculators on the attitudes and computational skills of children in grades four through seven (Doctoral dissertation, Arizona State University, 1976). *Dissertation Abstracts International*, 1976, *37*, 3382A-3383A. (University Microfilms No. 76-27,270)

Palmer, H. B. A. Minicalculators in the classroom — What do teachers think? *Arithmetic Teacher*, 1978, *25*(7), 27-28.

Quinn, D. R. Yes of no? Calculators in the classroom. *NASSP Bulletin*, 1976, 60(396), 77-80.

Shult, D. L. The effect of the hand-held calculator on arithmetic problem-solving abilities of sixth-grade students (Doctoral dissertation, University of Oregon, 1979). *Dissertation Abstracts International*, 1980.

Shumway, R. J. Hand calculators: Where do you stand? *Arithmetic Teacher*, 1976, *23*, 569-572.

Suydam, M. *Electronic hand calculators: The implications for pre-college education. Final report.* Washington, D.C.: National Science Foundation, 1976. (ERIC Document Reproduction Service No. ED 127 205)

Vaughn, L. R. A problem of the effects of hand-held calculators and a specially designed curriculum on attitude toward mathematics, achievement in mathematics, and retention of mathematical skills (Doctoral dissertation, University of Houston, 1976). *Dissertation Abstracts International*, 1977, *37*, 4938A-4939A. (University Microfilms No. 77-1,529)

Wajeeh, A. The effect of a program of meaningful and relevant mathematics on the achievement of the ninth grade general mathematics student (Doctoral dissertation, Wayne State University, 1976). *Dissertation Abstracts International*, 1976, *37*, 2801A-2802A. (University Microfilms No. 76-26,189)

Wheatley, G. H., Shumway, R. J., Coburn, T. G., Reys, R. E., Schoen, H. L., Wheatley, C. L., & White, A. L. Calculators in elementary schools. *Arithmetic Teacher*, 1979, *27*(1), 18-21.

Whitaker, W. H. A study of change in achievement, interest and attitudinal varieties accompanying the use of electronic calculators in a first grade mathematics curriculum (Doctoral dissertation, University of Southern California, 1977). *Dissertation Abstracts International*, 1977, *38*, 97A-98A.

REFERENCE NOTES

1. Suydam, M. N. *State-of-the-art review on calculators: Their use in education.* Columbus, Ohio: Calculator Information Center, April 1978.

2. Calculator Information Center. *Introduction to research on hand-held calculators, K-12,* (Bulletin No. 9). Columbus, Ohio: Calculator Information Center, August 1977.

3. Kelley, J. L., & Lansing, I. G. *Some implications of the use of hand calculators in mathematics instruction* (Paper prepared for the

Project on Problem Solving Strategies and the Use of Hand Calculators in the Elementary Schools). Unpublished manuscript, Indiana University, Mathematics Education Development Center, 1974.

4. McClintock, C. E. *The hand calculator as an algebra I problem solving tool*. Paper presented at the NCTM 56th Annual Meeting, San Diego, California, April 12-15, 1978.

APPENDIX A
The Metric System

Numbers are used to model (i.e., represent) things that can be counted or measured. A person is 67 years old; a distance is 145 km; a temperature is 18°C; a mass is 93 g; a volume is 17 l. A system of measurement uses units, such as years, seconds, metres, degrees Celsius, grams, and litres. The metric system is a scientifically designed and internally consistant system of units.

Most of the world outside of the United States uses the metric system. The United States began a transition to the metric system back in 1866, when the metre became the official unit of length. But acceptance has been very slow outside the scientific community. On December 23, 1975, President Gerald Ford signed the Metric Conversion Act of 1975. It declares that a change over to the metric system is national policy.

This voluntary changeover is proceeding slowly but steadily. New editions of textbooks are apt to be metric (that is, use metric units in problems). School systems have plans for a gradual conversion to metric instruction. The idea is that eventually only metric will be used in the schools.

As this transition goes on, teachers will need to be familiar with both the metric and the English system of units. In their daily lives outside of school they will still have to cope with pounds and ounces; miles, yards, feet and inches; gallons, quarts, and pints; degrees Fahrenheit. In school the teacher will use metres as a unit of length, litres as a unit of volume, grams as a unit of mass, and degrees Celsius to measure temperature. Prefixes such as milli, centi, deci, deka, hecto, and kilo are used to indicate multiplies of metres, litres, and grams.

It is not appropriate to teach conversions from metric to English units, or vise versa, in the elementary school. But a teacher should have some insight into solving conversion problems. Information useful to elementary teachers is given in the tables.

METRIC CHART

BASE UNIT	ADDED PREFIX	RESULTS	WRITTEN	WRITTEN	COMMONLY USED
	milli	millimetre	0.001 m	1 mm	Yes
	centi	centimetre	0.01 m	1 cm	Yes
	deci	decimetre	0.1 m	1 dm	No
metre		metre	m	m	Yes
	deka	dekametre	10 m	1 dam	No
	hecto	hectometre	100 m	1 hm	No
	kilo	kilometre	1000 m	1 km	Yes
	milli	millilitre	0.001 l	1 ml	Yes
	centi	centilitre	0.01 l	1 cl	No
	deci	decilitre	0.1 l	1 dl	No
litre		litre	l	l	Yes
	deka	dekalitre	10 l	1 dal	No
	hecto	hectolitre	100 l	1 hl	No
	kilo	kilolitre	1000 l	1 kl	No
	milli	milligram	0.001 g	1 mg	No
	centi	centigram	0.01 g	1 cg	No
	deci	decigram	0.1 g	1 dg	No
gram		gram	g	g	Yes
	deka	dekagram	10 g	1 dag	No
	hecto	hectogram	100 g	1 hg	No
	kilo	kilogram	1000 g	1 kg	Yes

CONVERSION FACTORS

1 metre = 39.370 inches

1 litre = 1.0567 quarts

1 kg = 2.2046 pounds

$$C = \frac{5}{9}(F - 32)$$

C = degrees Celsius

F = degrees Fahrenheit

Example: Find the ratio of the length of a mile to the length of a kilometre.

Solution: One needs a common unit of measure for each.

1 mile = 5280 feet = 63360 inches

1 km = 1000 m = 39370 inches

$$\text{Ratio} = \frac{63360 \text{ inches}}{39370 \text{ inches}} = 1.6093472$$

To two decimal place accuracy we conclude a mile is 1.61 km.

Example: An automobile gas tank holds 21 U.S. gallons. How many litres is this?

Solution: 21 gallons = 84 quarts
1 litre = 1.0567 quarts

$$\frac{84\ quarts}{1.0567\ quarts/litre} = 79.49276\ litres$$

Rounded to two decimal place accuracy we conclude 21 gallons = 79.49 litres.

Example: A U.S. ton is 2000 pounds. How many kg is this?

Solution: 1 ton = 2000 pounds
1 kg = 2.2046 pounds

$$\frac{2000\ pounds}{2.2046\ pounds/kg} = 907.19404\ kg$$

Rounded to the nearest whole number we conclude 1 ton = 907 kg.

Example: How many grams in a pound?

Solution: 1 kg = 1000 g = 2.2046 pounds

$$\frac{1000\ g}{2.2046\ pounds} = 453.59702\ g/pound$$

Rounded to the nearest whole number we conclude there are 454 grams in a pound.

APPENDIX B
Calculator Use in Schools

Douglas L. Shult

One of the most complex, controversial issues in mathematics education today is the use of hand-held calculators in schools. The complexity of this issue appears to stem from confusion among educators, parents, and calculator manufacturers over the calculator's role and purpose in the mathematics curriculum. Some view the calculator as an innovative, instructional aid capable of enriching and extending present curriculum goals. Others fear the calculator to be capable of devastating the school curriculum, transforming students into nonthinking, blurry-eyed button pushers. Without citing underlying research data, this appendix attempts (1) to present the basis for this dispute and (2) to identify types of calculator uses in school mathematics programs.

A common thread running through the controversy appears to be the fact that constituent groups hold vested interests. Currently, many teachers are recovering from the "false promises" of "modern mathematics" and are reluctant to place a great deal of faith in hand-held calculators as a curriculum innovation. They want to make sure that students fully understand fundamental arithmetical concepts before they allow them to use calculators. Parents want the best possible education for their children. In many cases this means schooling similar to their own which, obviously, did not include calculators. And, manufacturers want to sell calculators. They do this by making them attractive for school use.

To place the argument in its proper, academic perspective, several authors have attempted to summarize dispassionately both sides of the issue (Bell, Esty, Payne, & Suydam, 1977; Hawthorne, 1973; Machlowitz, 1976; Palmer, 1978; Quinn, 1976; Shumway, 1976). Advocates for the use of calculators in schools claim they (1) facilitate understanding and concept development; (2) aid in computation and problem solving; (3) motivate and encourage curiosity and independence; (4) aid in understanding algorithmic processes; (5) encourage estimation, approximation, and verification; and (6) most importantly, exist, and thus cannot be ignored. Opponents argue calculators (1) destroy all motivation for learning the basic facts, (2) discourage mathematical thinking, (3) cause a dependence on them for all calculations, (4) are inappropriate for slow learners, (5) block the opportunity to fully understand algorithmic process, and (6) develop the notion that mathematics is nothing more than pressing buttons on a black box.

At present no reliable information is available on the extent to which calculators are being used in schools. However, fragmentary results from a relatively few small-scale surveys reflect a pattern of increasing calculator availability to students. The Shawnee Mission (Kansas) Public Schools, for example, conducted one such survey of over 22,000 students. Results indicated that ownership of calculators on the part of elementary students increased 425% from 1975 to 1977, while access to calculators increased 35% (Suydam, Note 1).

As information is limited on the extent of calculator use in schools, so is data on the categories of calculator usage. Nevertheless, from information that is available, four types of uses are predominant in elementary and middle school classrooms:

1. Checking computational work done with paper and pencil.
2. Games, which may or may not have much to do with furthering the mathematical content, but do provide motivation.
3. Calculation: when numbers must be operated with, the calculator is used with the regular textbook or program.
4. Exploratory activities, leading to the development of calculator-specific activities where the calculator is used to teach mathematical ideas. (Suydam, Note 1, p. 4)

School districts, which use calculators and experiment with them, report that they are being put to one or more of the following uses:

1. The district or school purchases a small number of calculators, which are given to teachers for exploratory activities. This is followed by discussion and decision on whether the district or school should purchase more.
2. Remedial mathematics or Title I classes receive calculators for use with low achievers who have not previously learned computational skills well.
3. Calculators are placed in advanced science and mathematics classes in secondary schools.
4. Pilot studies and research are being conducted on the effect of

the use of calculators.

5. Teachers and students bring calculators into the classroom and use them when it seems feasible. (Bell, Esty, Payne & Suydam, 1977, p. 238)

It is evident from the foregoing discussion that there is divergent opinion concerning calculator use in schools. It is also clear that schools which choose to use them do so in many different and imaginative ways. Despite both the controversy over their use and the lack of any clear-cut universal procedure for incorporating them into classroom instruction, calculators are here to stay.

Students will increasingly discover ingenious ways to use them. Thus, teachers will need to become aware of and experienced in their productive use in the classroom. By studying the material and performing the exercises and applications contained in this book, you can gain the prerequisite knowledge and experience that is necessary to enrich and enliven your classroom with the magic of the hand-held calculator.

APPENDIX C

A Review of Research of Calculator Effects on Mathematical Abilities

Douglas L. Shult

This review of research on the relationship of the calculator to mathematical abilities is designed to give you a general understanding of the questions researchers are asking, the types of research being done, and the results. It is written, as much as possible, from an unbiased perspective. The purpose is to give you the necessary information for drawing your own generalizations and making your own conclusions about the effects of calculators on mathematical abilities.

Because the research separates nicely into two parts, it is reported under two major headings: (1) Calculator Effects on Attitudes, Achievement, and Computational Skills and (2) Calculator Effects on Ability to Solve Verbal Problems.

Calculator Effects on Attitudes, Achievement, and Computational Skills

Investigations of calculator effects on attitudes, achievement, and computation have been conducted with increasing frequency in recent years. Early researchers exclusively used hand-crank or electric desk-type calculators in their studies. However, with the advent of solid-state technology, calculator research studies have begun to emphasize the use of hand calculators. Therefore it seems logical and convenient to present the research reported in this section in two parts: (1) research pertaining to desk calculators and (2) research incorporating the use of hand-held calculators.

DESK CALCULATORS

One of the first studies which attempted to determine the influence of hand-crank calculating machines on arithmetic performance was conducted by Betts (1937). Treatment was a six-week program of drill and practice administered to 13 above-average sixth-grade mathematics students. Gain scores on four tests were compared; all subjects made positive gains. Research limitations of the study's one-group pretest-posttest design prevented Betts from making any authoritative conclusions. However, he was able to report that (1) during the study interest was at an all-time high and (2) because of gains on all tests, there was no loss of computational ability.

Fehr, McMeen and Sobel (1957) used similar hand-operated computing machines, a larger sample of fifth-grade students, and a pretest-posttest control-group design to study calculator effects on paper-and-pencil computation and arithmetic reasoning. Experimental students used machines to supplement regular textbook material, while control subjects covered the same syllabus without calculators. After four and one-half months, investigators found that subjects who used machines (1) gained more in reasoning ability, (2) gained more in computational ability, and (3) exhibited significantly better attitudes toward arithmetic than the control subjects. Durrance (1964) employed similar experimental and treatment techniques in an attempt to determine the effect of rotary calculators on achievement in arithmetic. Subjects were 70 average-ability sixth-, seventh-, and eighth-grade mathematics students matched according to IQ and arithmetic achievement. Contrary to the results of Fehr et al. (1957), Durrance found that calculators did not significantly enable students to achieve in arithmetic.

Attitude, achievement, and computational skill were among the five criterion variables Mastbaum (1969) sought to investigate by randomly assigning 171 slow-learning junior high school mathematics students to four treatments. F-ratio analysis of the data revealed that the electronic desk calculator, when used as a teaching aid, did not significantly improve attitude, increase mathematical ability, or improve noncalculator computational skill. Similar results were obtained by Cech (1972) in a seven-week experimental study using low-achieving ninth-grade mathematics students. Cech's experimental subjects used desk calculators to verify paper-and-pencil calculations; his control subjects did not use calculators.

Advani (1972) studied a single group of 18 severely limited (educable mentally retarded and neurologically impaired) subjects (age 12 to 15) for a six-month period in an attempt to assess the effects of desk calculator operation on achievement and attitude toward mathematics. Students worked individually and were encouraged to check their work on calculators. In contrast to the results of Mastbaum (1969) and Cech (1972), comparisons of pretest and posttest data indicated significant gains in mathematical achievement and attitudes. In addition, work with calculators reduced disruptive behavior. Because of control limitations in Advani's research design, results were viewed as suggestive and inconclusive.

In one of the most recent desk calculator studies, Gaslin (1975) attempted to compare the effects of two algorithm sets (conventional and calculator-based) on achievement and attitudes of 101 low-achieving ninth-grade general mathematics students. Calculator-based algorithm sets involved converting fractions to truncated decimals and performing indicated operations on the decimals using calculators. Three treatments were conducted for a ten-week period within a mastery-learning model. One-way NOVA and two-way ANCOVA revealed that (1) none of the treatments significantly improved attitudes toward mathematics; however, (2) calculator-based algorithm sets produced significantly greater computational skill than conventional algorithm sets. These findings seem to indicate that when arithmetic algorithms are adapted for use on the calculator, improvements in computational skill can be made.

The variety of experimental treatments and research designs reviewed in these desk calculator studies seem to account, in part, for the inconsistencies reported in some of the results. Although desk calculators do not appear to diminish mathematical attitudes, achievement, and computational skills, they do not, in general, ameliorate them. In view of these observations and in light of the expense, size, and weight of desk calculators, it is not difficult to understand why they never became permanent fixtures in mathematics classrooms.

HAND-HELD CALCULATORS

Hand calculators, on the other hand, seem to have produced quite different results. In a year-long study by Hawthorne and Sullivan (1975), 98 sixth-grade students participated in an experiment to determine how calculators could supplement, support, and enrich the regular program. Students used calculators along with the standard state adopted syllabus to check answers, develop algorithms, solve verbal problems, and explore relationships between common and decimal fractions. Posttest mean scores for concepts and computation were compared using the t-test for correlated means and found to favor calculator students at the .02 level of significance. Project personnel concluded that calculators are powerful computational aids and can be used to advantage in sixth-grade classes.

Jones (1976) used a group of 171 average-ability sixth-grade students to investigate the effects of hand-held calculators on mathematics achievement and attitude. Treatment extended over a nine-week period and consisted of routine arithmetic instruction. Experimental students used calculators; control subjects used paper and pencils exclusively. Findings indicated that calculator students demonstrated significant gains at the .001 level of confidence in computation, concepts, and total mathematics achievement. No significant differences were found in attitudes of students toward mathematics. Results reported by Jones, as well as Hawthorne and Sullivan (1975), tend to support the notion that calculators are more effective in developing computational skill and formulating mathematics concepts than paper and pencils only.

Using a sample of 126 average-ability sixth-grade mathematics students, Borden (1976) found that calculator usage made very little difference in mathematics achievement of specific concepts and skills in decimal fractions. Pretest-posttest analysis of investigator-made testing materials revealed that students using calculators and students not using calculators during instructional periods made significant gains in achievement at the .05 level of confidence. These gains on the part of both groups can be attributed, in part, (1) to the degree of validation of investigator-developed tests and (2) to the power of the instructional treatment which was written so as to precede or follow the study of common fractions and include or not include calculators.

Borden also reported that there was no significant change in attitude among students using calculators. However, students who did not use calculators demonstrated a significantly negative change in attitude toward mathematics. Borden reasoned that this change in attitude could have been affected by the fact that students not using calculators knew that other students in the same school were using calculators.

Achievement and attitude were among the dependent variables Vaughn (1976) sought to investigate in an eight-week study. Eight junior high general mathematics classes were randomly assigned to control and experimental treatments. Control groups received traditional classroom instruction while experimental groups received special curriculum which integrated the use of hand-held calculators. Multiple regression analysis on pretest-posttest data indicated that (1) there was a significant difference with respect to achievement at the 5% level in favor of the experimental group and (2) there was no significant difference between control and experimental groups with respect to attitude toward mathematics. Because experimental treatment incorporated the use of calculators as well as a substantially different curriculum from the one used in the control group, it cannot be concluded that calculators caused the significant increase in achievement demonstrated by the experimental group.

In a carefully controlled 15-week experiment whose purpose was to determine effects of calculators on achievement and attitudes of ninth-grade general mathematics students, Wajeeh (1976) found that students who used calculators scored significantly higher ($p < .05$) on tests of computation than students who did not use calculators. Calculator users, however, did not significantly improve their concept, total mathematics, or attitude scores. Similar results were observed by Hutton (1976) who studied calculator effects on ninth-grade algebra students.

Nelson (1976) used a pretest-posttest nonequivalent control group design with a sample of 196 fourth-, fifth-, sixth-, and seventh-grade students for a 12-week period to evaluate calculator effects on basic computational skills and attitudes toward mathematics. In contrast to the results of Jones (1976), Borden (1976), Vaughn (1976), Wajeeh (1976), and Hutton (1976), Nelson (1976) found that attitudes can be significantly improved with hand calculators are used to supplement the regular curriculum. Nelson also found that significant gains in computational skill can be made by students who utilize hand calculators. This latter finding was consistent with the majority of results reported in this section.

Hand-held calculator research in education to date has primarily focused on the calculator's relationship to mathematical achievement, attitude toward mathematics, and development of computational skill. Most studies have involved comparisons among groups of students who use or do not use calculators. The Calculator Information Center (Note2) reported the major findings of 29 such studies. Of the 40 findings noted, 19 were cases in which calculator groups achieved significantly higher than paper-and-pencil subjects, 18 were instances of no significant differences, and three were cases in which noncalculator students made significantly higher scores. Such global tabulation provides some support for the belief that calculators can promote achievement and improve skills.

Undoubtedly, the most useful skill in mathematics is the ability to solve problems. The next section presents an analysis of research which examines the relationship of the hand calculator to the process of problem solving.

Calculator Effects on Ability to
Solve Verbal Problems

In one of the earliest calculator studies available, Betts (1937) attempted to investigate the effects of calculating machine practice on sixth-grade students' problem-solving techniques. Betts saw quite clearly that when calculators are used in mathematical problem solving, the stress and emphasis is placed where it should be — on process analysis. Because calculators minimize time-consuming computations, he hypothesized that students solve problems more efficiently, more accurately, and deliberate more on the analysis of problems rather than on computations needed for solutions. Although Betts' observations did not contribute significantly to the knowledge of calculator effects on techniques for problem analysis, he was among the first to identify the area as fertile ground for educational research and thus to acknowledge the interface between modern technology and human problem-solving thought process.

In the decades to follow, because of the expense and awkwardness of desk calculators, few researchers explored the relationship of computing machines to mathematical problem solving. It was not until the advent of inexpensive pocket calculators and the interest in their potential use in schools that educational conferences, study groups, and individual researchers once again began to make recommendations for needed research.

One of the most notable of these recommendations came from the National Advisory Committee on Mathematical Education (1975). The foundations for these recommendations were laid by Kelley and Lansing (Note 3) in a paper prepared for the Indiana University project on "Problem Solving Strategies and the Use of Hand Calculators in the Elementary Schools." Tentative conclusions reached in this paper were the following:

1. Several sorts of learning processes and problem-solving techniques seem more likely to occur to students using hand calculators.

2. Numerical exploration is enormously easier and quicker using hand calculators.

3. Freedom from the distraction of mechanical detail accelerates the mathematical learning process.

4. Facility and accuracy in straightforward algorithmic calculation is subordinate to deliberation required for accurately pushing buttons on a calculator.

5. The role of the calculator is to minimize computational digression so that attention can be given to understanding the conceptual framework of a problem.

Although these conclusions seem to be grounded in the same rationale as the one presented by Betts, one important difference is that Kelley and Lansing were able to precipitate recommendations which motivated an interest in conducting needed research.

Several investigators have used experimental designs and

standardized tests to study the relationship of hand calculators to mathematical problem solving. Boling (1977) performed such a calculator-based investigation with high school general mathematics students. He found that computation performed on the hand-held calculator did not positively or negatively affect verbal problem-solving ability. In an experimental study using average-ability junior high mathematics students, Andersen (1976) found subjects using hand calculators solved problems correctly at almost twice the rate of subjects not using calculators. He concluded that calculators, indeed, had a positive effect on problem-solving ability. Whitaker (1977) conducted an experimental investigation using average-ability first graders. He found that students who used calculators to check paper-and-pencil calculations performed consistently higher in the solution of verbal problems than students who did not have access to calculators.

Few researchers have dealt specifically with the problem of examining calculator effects on the process dimension of problem solving. McClintock (Note 4) performed such a study using a group of 36 above-average ninth-grade algebra students. A combined experimental/clinical-behavioral research design incorporated three treatment groups. Each received differential problem solving and calculator instruction. Protocols of individual preinterviews and postinterviews utilizing the *Thinking-Aloud Technique* were analyzed for process differences. Analysis of protocols revealed that calculator groups demonstrated more stability in the use of arithmetic algorithms and guessing-and-checking techniques than in the use of productive-inferences and algebraic-equations processes. McClintock concluded that intensive problem-solving instruction which incorporates the use of calculators facilitates achievement in algebra.

In another experimental study, Shult (1979) used a group of 30 average sixth-grade arithmetic students to determine calculator effects on process and product dimensions of problem solving. Subjects received six-weeks of identical individualized problem-solving instruction in two groups. Experimental subjects employed hand calculators to perform all computations, while control subjects were required to use paper and pencil. Responses from individual interviews, in which subjects "thought aloud" about solutions to word problems, were analyzed for process and product differences. Analysis of differences in preinterview-postinterview gain scores between groups revealed that subjects who used calculators required the same amount of time to solve word problems, were no more nor less accurate in their answers, and were as inclined to check answers as subjects who used paper and pencils to solve problems. In addition, the calculator group made about as many errors constructing logical problem-solving strategies, employed neither a broader nor more restricted range of problem-solving processes, and used trial-and-error strategies with about the same frequency as the no-calculator group. From these results, Shult reasoned that hand-held calculators neither positively nor negatively influence the problem-solving effectiveness of average sixth-grade students. In addition, Shult concluded that calculators do not appear to produce significant differences in the processes and strategies employed to solve word problems.

Other researchers have examined the effects of calculator use in mathematics classrooms over longer periods of time. Their results tend to corroborate Shult's findings. In a year-long study conducted with 1,500 students in grades two through six in five midwestern states, Wheatley et al. (1979) found that standardized tests of attitudes, basic facts, concepts, and applications produced no significant differences between calculator and no-calculator groups. Nevertheless, these results together with many observations made during the course of the study prompted Wheatley et al. to conclude that calculators are an excellent aid for developing problem-solving skill, that they may make possible a broader range of process and strategies, and that students who use them are not limited to solving problems which contain "nice" numbers.

As the preceding review indicates, evidence of the relationship of calculators to attitudes, achievement, computational skills, and verbal problem solving is not conclusive. However, there seems to be some support for the belief that calculators do not cause measurable detrimental effects on the teaching and learning of mathematics. Indeed, some researchers conclude that calculators contribute significantly to positive mathematics attitudes and enhance the successful learning of computational skills and problem-solving processes.

APPENDIX D

Glossary

ALGEBRAIC LOGIC CALCULATOR   A calculator which accepts instructions in algebraic notation order. Such a calculator has an $\boxed{=}$ key. It calculates the sum 8 + 13 when one pushes the key sequence $\boxed{8}\ \boxed{+}\ \boxed{1}\ \boxed{3}\ \boxed{=}$.

ALGORITHM   A step by step set of mathematical directions guaranteed to solve a specified type of problem. Grade school students learn paper and pencil algorithms for addition, subtraction, multiplication, and division. Many algorithms can be carried out by calculators or computers.

ARTIFICIAL INTELLIGENCE   The branch of computer science that deals with the question of how "smart" a computer is or can be. It includes the study of computerized game playing, medical diagnosis, language translation, question answering, and conversation.

BASIC   *Beginners All-purpose Symbolic Instruction Code.* A programming language developed at Dartmouth University and currently the most widely used programming language in elementary and secondary schools. It was designed to be easy for students to learn how to use.

BUG   An error in hardware or in software of a calculator or computer. The detection and correction of errors is called debugging.

CALCULATOR   A device for the input, storage, manipulation, and output of numbers. An inexpensive hand-held calculator is small, battery powered, and can perform the operations $+$, $-$, $\times$, and $\div$. More expensive calculators have additional memory, more built-in functions (operations), and may be programmable.

CALCULATOR ARITHMETIC   The calculator number system is different than the real number system. An 8-digit calculator performs arithmetic on this system, truncating or rounding answers to eight digits. This truncated or rounded arithmetic, called calculator arithmetic, is similar to the arithmetic performed by a computer.

CALCULATOR FUNCTION   A mathematical function built into the calculator circuitry. A 4-function calculator contains circuitry to perform the functions addition, subtraction, multiplication, and division. Examples of functions often built into calculator circuitry include $\sqrt{\ }$, %, x^2, and x^y.

CALCULATOR NUMBER LINE   The number line for an 8-digit calculator that does not use scientific notation contains a finite number of points, extends from -99999999 to $+99999999$, and the points are not equally spaced. Thus it is quite different than the real number line.

CELSIUS   Temperature in the metric system is measured in degrees Celsius, °C. Under conditions of standard pressure water boils at 100°C and freezes at 0°C. Celsius is related to the Fahrenheit temperature scale by the formula $C = 5(F - 32)/9$.

CHAIN CALCULATION   A calculation involving a sequence of two or more operations, such as $5 + 8 - 9$ or $6 \times 7 + 4$.

CHARACTER   A digit, letter, punctuation mark, or other symbol. A computer is designed to work with an extensive character set, rather than just digits. A computer's primary storage is often stated in characters, such as a 16,000 character memory.

CHIP   Electronic components such as transistors and resistors can be manufactured on a small piece, or chip, of silicone. With current technology a single chip, less than a cm on a side, may contain tens of thousands of electronic components. This technology has made possible inexpensive and small electronic calculators and computers.

CLEAR   The CLEAR key, usually labeled C on a calculator, changes the contents of certain memory locations to zero and sets the Operation location to "none."

CLEAR ENTRY   The CLEAR ENTRY key, usually labeled CE, sets the number currently being keyed in to zero. It is used to correct an error. On some calculators CE also allows one to change the Operation to be performed.

COBOL   A widely used, business-oriented language. The name comes from the longer name *Common Business Oriented Language*. It was developed in 1960 to meet the specific needs of people engaged in business data processing.

COMPUTER   A machine consisting of hardware and software for the input, storage, manipulation, and output of information coded as characters. It is designed to rapidly and automatically follow a detailed step-by-step set of directions, a program, stored in its memory.

COMPUTER ASSISTED INSTRUCTION   The use of a computer as an instructional delivery system.

DISC or DISK   A secondary storage device for computers consisting of one or more flat circular plates coated with magnetic iron oxide. A modern disk pack may consist of up to 20 recording surfaces in a single unit, and may store well over 500 million characters. Access to any part of the disk by the read/write mechanism may be less than 1/10 second.

EIGHT-DIGIT CALCULATOR   An electronic calculator designed to accept as input, store, calculate with, and display numbers of up to eight digits in length.

EQUATION   A mathematical statement of equality between two or more quantities. Examples include $5 + 2 = 7$ and $A = lw$. The latter type of equation is called a Formula.

FLOATING POINT ARITHMETIC   A type of scientific notation arithmetic used by most calculators and computers. The machine stores a number by its significant digits and an appropriate power of 10. Calculations are automatically performed to full machine accuracy.

FLOWCHART   A two dimensional diagram, making use of various shaped boxes and connecting lines, giving a detailed set of directions. A flowchart is often used in the calculator or computer field to represent a plan for solving a particular type of problem.

FORMULA   An equation involving one or more variables.

FUNCTION   A mathematical mapping from one set (called the domain) into another set (called the range). Often the domain consists of single numbers. The square root function has the non-negative real numbers as its domain, and the non-negative real numbers as its range. The addition function, usually denoted by $+$, has pairs of real numbers as its domain and the real numbers as its range. See Calculator Function.

FUNCTION KEYS   Calculator keys such as $\boxed{+}$, $\boxed{-}$, $\boxed{\times}$, $\boxed{\div}$, $\boxed{M+}$, $\boxed{M-}$, $\boxed{\sqrt{\ }}$, $\boxed{\%}$, $\boxed{1/x}$. Each corresponds to a built-in function the calculator is designed to perform.

GRAM   A metric measure of mass. The mass of 1 cm³ of distilled water at 4°C. The words mass and weight are often mistakenly used interchangeably. Weight is a measure of the pull of gravity upon a mass. Under zero gravity conditions a mass has no weight.

HARDWARE   The physical machinery and circuitry of a calculator or computer. A computer system consists of both hardware and software (computer programs).

INFORMATION RETRIEVAL   A branch of computer science dealing with the computerized storage and retrieval of information.

INTEGRATED CIRCUIT   An electronic circuit containing a number of transistors, resistors, and other components. Often called a Chip.

KILOGRAM   One thousand grams. The mass of one litre of distilled water at 4° C.

LCD   Liquid crystal display. A type of calculator display that depends upon reflected light and uses very little electrical energy. A LCD calculator's batteries may last for 1,000 to 2,000 hours or more of usage.

LED   Light emitting diode. A type of calculator display that uses small lights, very visible in dim light. The drain on batteries is relatively large, so a set of batteries in a LED calculator may last for less than a dozen hours of usage.

LINE PRINTER   A computer-driven printer that prints an entire line nearly simultaneously. Printing speeds of 300 to 2000 lines per minute are common. Such a printer is hundreds of times as fast as a human typist.

LITRE   A metric measure of volume or capacity equal to 1,000 cm^3. This is the same as a cube 10 cm on a side.

LOGO   A computer programming language developed by Seymour Papert at MIT for use by grade school students.

MASS   The terms "mass" and "weight" have been used as synonyms by some people. Mass is the amount of matter in an object and is measured in grams or submultiples or multiples thereof. Weight refers to the gravitational force on an object and is measured in newtons, a unit of force.

MATHEMATICAL MODEL   The use of mathematical symbols and notation to represent certain aspects of a problem or system. Formulas such as $P = 2l + 2w$ for the perimeter of a rectangle, and $E = mc^2$ relating mass to energy, are examples of models.

MEMORY   Storage space in a calculator or computer. Memory is used to store data being processed (for example, numbers), operations to be performed, and programs.

METRE   The basic unit of length in the metric system. Defined as 1,650,763.73 wave lengths in a vacuum of the orange-red line of the spectrum of krypton$_{86}$. The symbol for metre is "m."

METRIC SYSTEM   A system of measurement using metres for length, grams for mass, litres for volume, and degrees Celsius for temperature. This system is used throughout the world and is gradually gaining acceptance in the United States.

MICROCOMPUTER   A computer whose central processing unit consists of a microprocessor, a single chip. Also used to refer to any inexpensive computer. Hundreds of thousands of microcomputers have been sold to use in homes and schools, with prices starting at $400 or so for a complete system.

OVERFLOW   The calculator number line is limited in length. When an answer produced by a calculator falls outside the range of this number line an overflow is said to have occurred. Most calculators signify an overflow error by displaying an E or by some other message on the display.

PASCAL   A computer programming language designed by computer scientists for instructional and problem solving purposes. It embodies many of the ideas of language design that were developed after earlier programming languages such as FORTRAN, COBOL, and BASIC came into widespread use.

PRIMITIVE   A problem that a person can solve immediately and easily, without deep thought. Not all people have the same primitives, and one's primitives change via education and practice. Access to a calculator with $\sqrt{}$ key makes square root into a primitive for a person.

PROGRAM   A detailed step by step set of instructions written in a language a machine can follow. Also, the process of preparing such a set of instructions.

PROGRAMMABLE CALCULATOR   A calculator designed so that a person can input a program and the machine can automatically execute the instructions in the program.

RPN   Reverse Polish Notation. A type of mathematical notation often used on the more expensive calculators designed to solve advanced engineering, science, and business problems. An RPN calculator can be recognized by the absence of an $\boxed{=}$ key and the presence of an $\boxed{\text{ENT}}$ or $\boxed{\text{ENTER}}$ key. To add 5 to 12 on such a calculator one keys in $\boxed{5}$ $\boxed{\text{ENT}}$ $\boxed{1}$ $\boxed{2}$ $\boxed{+}$.

ROUND A process of approximating a given number to a specified number of digits. To round a positive integer to the nearest hundred one examines the 10's digit. If it is 4 or less, the last two digits of the given number are changed to zeros. If it is 5 or higher the last two digits of the given number are changed to zeros but the hundreds digit is increased by 1. Thus 637 rounded to the nearest hundred is 600 while 653 rounds to 700.

ROUNDING ERROR The process of approximating a number by rounding usually introduces an error, the difference between the original number and its approximation. This is called a rounding error.

SCIENTIFIC NOTATION The representation of a number by a decimal fraction part times a power of 10. In scientific notation one writes 69257 as 6.9257×10^4, and .00381 as 3.81×10^{-3}.

SOFTWARE Programs for a calculator or a computer. These are essential to the operation of a programmable calculator or a computer. A collection of software is called a program library or library.

TRUNCATE A process of approximating a given number to a specified number of digits. All digits to the right of the specified point are set to zero. Thus both 637 and 653, when truncated to the nearest hundred, give 600 as the resulting approximation.

TRUNCATION ERROR The process of approximating a number by truncation usually introduces an error, the difference between the original number and its approximation. This is called a truncation error, and is common in calculator arithmetic.

UNDERFLOW A calculator number line contains points (i.e., numbers) immediately above and below zero. For an 8-digit calculator that does not use scientific notation these numbers are $-.0000001$ and $+.0000001$. When the calculator produces a non-zero answer inside this range it will truncate it to zero. (If it is a calculator that rounds when answers inside the range $-.00000005$ to $+.00000005$ will round to zero.) The result is called an underflow, or an underflow error. Most calculators do not give an error indication when this occurs. A calculator user can often detect such an error by observing that an answer of zero unexpectedly has been produced.

VIDEODISC A disc designed to store television pictures and to be played by a television videodisc player. With current technology one side of a single disk, about the size of a typical 33 rpm record, stores 30 minutes of television. This is 54,000 individual pictures. Videodisc technology, when combined with a microcomputer, makes possible relatively inexpensive and high quality computer assisted instruction.

Answers to Exercises

Chapter 2

Set 2.2 2. Test A (1) 6,524, (2) 5,391, (3) 234, (4) 1,080, (5) 330, (6) 1,644.1$\overline{6}$, (7) 121, (8) 82,625, (9) 17,100, (10) 151, Test B (1) 4,890, (2) 2,391, (3) 152, (4) 930, (5) 456, (6) 1,345.8, (7) 391, (8) 64,195, (9) 18,400, (10) 268.

Set 2.3 1. (a) 4, (b) 4, (c) 22, (d) 1, (e) 30, (f) 4, (g) 62, (h) 13; 2. (a) 31, (b) 4, (c) 27, (d) 137, (e) 40, (f) 2, (g) 30, (h) 27, (i) 26, (j) 10, (k) 25, (l) 10, (m) 1, (n) 11, (o) 65, (p) 37; 3. (a) 3, (b) 8, (c) 9, (d) 1,000, (e) 32, (f) 25; 4. (a) 1, $^-$3, (b) 3, $^-$3⅓, (c) 7, $^-$8, (d) 4, (e) 3; 5. (a) 5, (b) 9, (c) 11, (d) 19, (e) 145.

Set 2.4 1. (a) 20,479, (b) 2,914.275, (c) 12.$\overline{108}$, (d) 83.55; 2. (a) 90.5, wrong operation, (b) 141, reversed digits, (c) 8,174, two sixes, (d) 25, wrong order of operations, (e) 1.$\overline{3}$, divided in wrong order, (f) 37,840, only one four, (g) 10.$\overline{18}$, reversed digits; 3. e-b-g-f-a-c-d.

Chapter 3

Set 3.1 1. (a) A = 28 sq cm, P = 22 cm, (b) A = 3,003.240 sq mm, P = 224.594 mm; 4. $19.28.

Set 3.4 1. 13 marbles; 2. $1.53; 3. $0.58; 4. $82.08; 5. $64.45; 6. 2.738 ⩽ n < 2.7304; 7. (a) 360°, (b) 360°, (c) 540°, (d) 720°, (e) 3,240°; 13. four-function calculator gives: (a) 0.74$\overline{9}$, (b) 1.08$\overline{3}$, (c) 0.5, (d) 0.1$\overline{6}$; 14. 3:46:40, Tuesday, PM; 15. March 11, 10:40, AM.

Set 3.5 1. 23; 2. 82; 3. 317; 4. 3,162; 5. (a) 2.65, (b) 13.00, (c) 2.35, (d) 6.00; 6. 3.21, 7.79; 7. (a) 2.58, 12.42, (b) 6.71, $^-$6.71, (c) 2.57.

Chapter 4

Set 4.1 1. A = 24.48 sq km, P = 21.2 km; 2. A = 161.29 sq mm, P = 50.8 mm; 3. 18.55 km; 4. 3.65 km/hr; 5. $4.13; 6. $4.25; 7. 204 in; 8. 259,200 sec; 9. $50.59; 10. 31.5 cm; 11. 10.$\overline{1}$ km/l; 12. C = 62.83 cm, A = 314.16 sq cm; 13. 201.06 cm, 497.36 revolutions, 482.29 revolutions; 14. 6.25 cm.

Set 4.2 1. A = 49,920 sq m, P = 12,815.6 m; 2. A = 3,654,000 sq m, C = 42,000.36 m; 3. $176.18; 4. $6.48; 5. 20°C, 98.6°F; 6. 7.75 m; 7. 4.9 m, 44.1 m, 176.4 m, 7.8 sec; 8. 9.74 m/sec, 29.22 m/sec, 58.44 m/sec, 76.21 m/sec; 9. 2.86 sec, 27.83 m/sec; 10. 2.74 mi; 11. 225.83 mi; 12. 4.38 km; 13. 178.90 km.

Set 4.3 2. (a) 5, (b) 0, (c) error; 3. (a) 0.05, (b) $0.\bar{3}$, (c) $^-0.\bar{3}$, (d) error;
4. (a) nonnegative real numbers, (b) real numbers, (c) real numbers
for dividend and nonzero real numbers for divisor; 7. (a) A =
221.6707 sq cm, C = 52.778757 cm, (b) A = 66,051.986 sq cm,
C = 991.06188 cm, (c) A = 12.192207 sq mm, C = 12.377875 mm,
(d) A = 0.0000578 sq cm, C = 0.0270176 cm, (e) eight-digit calculator gives: A = error, 10-digit calculator gives: A = 1,963,495,409
sq m, C = 157,079.63 m, (f) A = 49,714,083 sq m, C = 24,994.511 m.

Set 4.4 1. P (l,w) = 2l + 2w, l(P,w) = (P − 2w)/2, w(P,l) = (P − 2l)/2;
2. A(l,w) = lw, l(A,w) = A/w, w(A,l) = A/l; 3. C(F) = ⅝(F − 32),
F(C) = ⅝C + 32; 6. V increases by factor of 8, S increases by factor
of 4; 7. A increases by factor of 4, C increases by factor of 2.

Set 4.5 1. eight-digit calculator gives: (a) 3.0000003, (b) 3.0000001,
(c) 6, (d) 6; 2. 0.000001, undefined, 0; 3. top down: 100.00000, bottom
up: 100.00001, exact answers: 100.00001; 9. $(12,345)^2$ = 152,399,020
(approx.), (a) 9,754,525,200, (b) 5,121,264,300, (c) 4,309,323,700,
(d) 321,759,110,000, (e) 11,628.765, (f) $14,132.\bar{2}$; 10. 5,878,612,800,000.

Chapter 5

Set 5.2 4. (a) $121.99, (b) $142.32, (c) $13.10, (d) $51.44; 6. (a) 33,766.85,
(b) 73,628.477, (c) 9,426,380.9; 9. (a) 4, (b) 0.1903, (c) 1; 10. (a) $59.78,
(b) $80.52, (c) $63.41, $94.23, (d) $59.55, $79.69, $62.99, $92.55.

Set 5.3 1. (a) 102.18, (b) $^-$309.5; 4. (a) 12.72, (b) 5.76, (c) 10.72, (d) 43.99;
5. 2.9289681 (both ways); 6. (a) $^-$0.0380953, (b) 1.7154214; 7. (a) 5,
(b) $^-$32, (c) 0, (d) 72, (e) 39; 8.00 (a) 0.85, (b) 5.45, (c) 0.21; 10. 0.38.

Set 5.4 1.

N	G	N/G	A = ½(G + N/G)
9	1	9	5
9	5	1.8	3.4
0	3.4	2.6470588	3.0235294
9	3.0235294	2.9766537	3.0000915
9	3.0000915	2.9999085	3.

2. (a) 4.125, 4.123106, 4.1231056, (b) 9, 5.444444, 4.2834466,
(c) 50.085, 25.212211, 12.943243.

Chapter 6

Set 6.1 4. (a) goose, (b) Boise, (c) hogs, (d) log, (e) bills, (f) shell, (g) beg, (h) bells, (i) sleigh, (j) bees.

Set 6.4 5. (a) (i) 27, (ii) 256, (iii) 47.045881, (iv) 68.671985, (v) 153.76, (vi) 2,281.4651, (b) (i) 6, (ii) 4, (iii) 2, (iv) 11, (v) 2, (vi) 5, (c) (i) $x \geq 4$, (ii) $x \geqslant 11$, (iii) $x \geqslant 24$, (d) (i) 5, (ii) 1, (iii) 2.

Set 6.5 1. (a) 100, 120, (b) 170, 180, (c) 1,400, 1,500, (d) 10,000, 11,000, (e) 1,900, 1,900; 2. (a) 400, (b) 900, (c) 13,000, (d) 6,000; 3. (a) 500, 600, 600, (b) 3,000, 3,000, 3,000, (c) 500, 500, 500, (d) 76, 86, 90, (e) 40, 50, 0; 4. (a) 2,100, (b) 5,600,000, (c) 450,000, (d) 10,800, (e) 120,000,000; 5. (a) 30, (b) 100, (c) 200, (d) 20, (e) 50.

Set 6.6 1. (a) 0.5, (b) $0.\overline{3}$, (c) 0.25, (d) 0.2, (e) $0.1\overline{6}$, (f) $0.\overline{6}$, (g) 0.5, (h) 0.4, (i) $0.\overline{3}$, (j) 0.75, (k) 0.6, (l) 0.5, (m) 0.8, (n) $0.\overline{6}$, (o) $0.8\overline{3}$; 2. (a) 1.5, (b) 8.5, (c) $4.\overline{3}$, (d) $13.\overline{3}$, (e) $5.1\overline{6}$, (f) 8.8, (g) 14.75, (h) 2.2, (i) $6.8\overline{3}$, (j) 4.75, (k) 7.25, (l) $12.\overline{6}$; 3. (b) 3/20, 6/40, (c) 1/4, 2/8, (d) 2/3, 4/6, (e) 2/5, 4/10, (f) 5/6, 10/12, (g) 3/4, 6/8, (h) 18/1, 36/2, (i) 1/10, 2/20, (j) 1/7, 2/14, (k) 3/7, 6/14; 4. (b) 1/5, (c) 1/2, (d) 3/4, (e) 3/5, (f) 1/10, (g) 4/5, (h) 7/20, (i) 9/20; 5. (a) 2/9, (b) 5/9, (c) 1/9, (d) 8/9, (e) 7/9, (f) 1/3, 9/9, 1; 6. (b) $8\frac{1}{9}$, (c) $2\frac{7}{9}$, (d) $15\frac{2}{9}$, (e) $3\frac{1}{3}$, (f) $66\frac{2}{3}$, (g) $9\frac{5}{9}$; 7. (a) 1/99, (b) 5/99, (c) 4/33, (d) 5/11, (e) 98/99, (f) 10/99, (g) 50/99, (h) 56/99, (i) 1/3.

Set 6.7 1. (a) 1.0822×10^{15}, (b) 1.2193×10^{17}, (c) 7.8073×10^{25}, (d) 9.6342×10^{26}.

Set 7.1 2. (a) 5, 25, 125, 625, 3,125, 15,625, 78,125, 390,625, 1,953,125, all fives, 5, (b) 2, 4, 8, 16, 32, 64, 128, 256, 512, (2, 4, 8, 6), 6, (c) 7, 49, 343, 2,401, 16,807, 177,649, 823,543, 5,764,801, 40,353,607, (7, 9, 3, 1), 1, (d) 2, 7, 0; 3. 1.0000500; 6. (a) 21, 34, 55, 89, 144, 233, 377, 610, 987, 1,597, (b) 1.6, 1.625, 1.6153846, 1.6190476, 1.617647, $1.61\overline{8}$, 1.6179775, 1.6180555, 1.6189257, 1.6189371, 1.6189327, 1.6180344, 0.0000005 (difference); 8. (a) 192, (b) 325, (c) 1,600, (d) 252, (e) 500,500; 9. 210, 5,050, 31,375, 500,500; 10. (a) 385, (b) 1,100, (c) 2,485.

Set 7.5 1. \$43.20, no; 2. $208.\overline{3}$ days, 7.35 days; 4. 9.2234×10^{18}, 1.8447×10^{19}, 5. \$653,120.00; 6. (a) 968,000 kg, (b) 168.48 km; 7. 16.73 hrs; 8,588.24 days, 219,117.65 days.

Chapter 8

Set 8.1   3.

Date	Deposit	Interest	Balance
1 January 1980	$1,000.00	— —	$ 1,000.00
1 April 1980	$1,000.00	$ 15.00	$ 2,015.00
1 July 1980	$1,000.00	$ 30.22	$ 3,045.22
1 October 1980	$1,000.00	$ 45.68	$ 4,090.90
1 January 1981	$1,000.00	$ 61.36	$ 5,152.26
1 April 1981	$1,000.00	$ 77.28	$ 6,229.54
1 July 1981	$1,000.00	$ 93.44	$ 7,322.98
1 October 1981	$1,000.00	$109.84	$ 8,432.82
1 January 1982	$1,000.00	$126.49	$ 9,559.31
1 April 1982	$1,000.00	$143.39	$10,702.70
1 July 1982	$1,000.00	$160.54	$11,863.24
1 October 1982	$1,000.00	$177.95	$13,041.19

4671-7
5-29